*Yes, I*
# COULD
*Care Less*

ALSO BY BILL WALSH

*Lapsing Into a Comma*
*The Elephants of Style*

# Yes, I COULD Care Less

## HOW TO BE A LANGUAGE SNOB WITHOUT BEING A JERK

## Bill Walsh

 ST. MARTIN'S GRIFFIN  NEW YORK

www.stmartins.com

Library of Congress Cataloging-in-Publication Data

Walsh, Bill (William F.)
    Yes, I could care less : how to be a language snob without being a jerk / Bill Walsh.—1st St. Martin's Griffin Edition.
        p. cm.
    Includes index.
    ISBN 978-1-250-00663-9 (trade paperback)
    ISBN 978-1-250-03201-0 (e-book)
    1. English language—Style—Handbooks, manuals, etc.   2. English language—Usage—Handbooks, manuals, etc.   3. English language—Grammer—Handbooks, manuals, etc.   I. Title.
    PE1460.W229 2013
    808'.042–dc23                                                    2013009317

St. Martin's Griffin books may be purchased for educational, business, or promotional use. For information on bulk purchases, please contact Macmillan Corporate and Premium Sales Department at 1-800-221-7945 extension 5442 or write specialmarkets@macmillan.com.

First Edition: June 2013

10  9  8  7  6  5  4  3  2  1

*For Terance and Kenneth.*
*Sorry I led you down this path.*

# Contents

## PART TWO ✳ In Practice

## PART THREE ✳ In Good Fun

# PART FOUR ❋ In Conclusion

# Acknowledgments

This book would not exist without Janet Rosen and Daniela Rapp—literally, if I may use *literally* literally.

Janet, my agent at Sheree Bykofsky Associates, had been after me to write a third book but had been stymied time and time again by my fundamental laziness. Enter Daniela, patron saint of language-book authors at St. Martin's Press. While I was minding my own business in Washington, D.C., Janet and Daniela were spending a lunch or two 227 miles to the north hatching a plan to get me off my butt. Eventually, they succeeded. I'm glad they did.

So I must thank Janet (and Sheree) and Daniela and the rest of the team at St. Martin's Griffin. I am also indebted to my colleagues at the *Washington Post*, in the American Copy Editors Society and in the online arguing-about-language community. Those colleagues are an invaluable source of ideas and inspiration, as are the copy editors who happen to be my brothers, Terence Walsh and Kenneth Walsh, and the Postie who happens to be my wife, Jacqueline Dupree.

# Introduction

These are interesting times for word nerds. We ate, shot and left, bonding over a joke about a panda and some rants about green-grocers who abuse apostrophes. A couple of young men took Lynne Truss's aversion to substandard signage a step further and documented a vandalism spree across America. We can go on Facebook and vow to judge people when they use poor grammar. The 50th anniversary of the publication of *The Elements of Style* inspired sentimental rever-ies. Grammar Girl's tally of Twitter followers is well into six digits. We can't get enough of a parody of the *Associated Press Stylebook*, of all things, or a collection of "unnecessary" quotation marks.

You might think all this interest in English usage would hearten the smartest people in the room, the men and women of linguistics. But you'd be wrong. Click away from the Fake AP Stylebook tweets for a moment and check in on a Web site called Language Log, where you'll learn that caring less and not caring less are, in fact, the same thing, and have been for decades. Same with literally and not liter-ally. Copy editors? Morons. *The Elements of Style*? A "little piece of trash."

Mercy! But the learned spoilsports have a point, up to a point. Strunk and White did offer up some rules that they didn't follow (and that we shouldn't, either). Language does evolve, it does sometimes defy logic, and it does depend on context. Different words can mean the same thing, and the same word can mean different things. You can almost always tell what *I could care less* means, and you're not likely to call in the fire brigade if you hear about someone's head *literally* exploding. Copy editors, I admit, *do* sometimes do dumb things.

The spoilsports have something in common with Arthur Fonzarelli, a.k.a. Fonzie, a.k.a. the Fonz. The Fonz, for those of you without advanced age or access to *Happy Days* reruns, was famously unable to say the word *wrong*. In Fonzie's case, he couldn't admit his own faults. He would get as far as "Wrrr—" but couldn't bring himself to finish the syllable. For the spoilsports, it's all those stickler bugaboos that they are loath to label with the *wr-* word. (Or are they *loathe?* Whatever. They wouldn't call it *wrrr—*.) They would rather not pet our peeves, thank you. Double negatives are fine because French uses both *ne* and *pas* to form a negative. Using words to mean the opposite of what they mean is fine because notables from Shakespeare to Hemingway did so. Subject-verb disagreement is fine because it's an example of a different dialect. The words that some people insist are not words—*irregardless, heighth, supposably*—are simply *nonstandard*. All of the above and more are fine, moreover, because the intent of the speaker/writer is understood perfectly well by the listener/reader. In some sense, *common error* is an oxymoron. Language change is inevitable, so why not lie back and enjoy it?

Still, whether you or I or the linguists like it or not, the cutting edge can be a dangerous place. We can't ignore the new, but we dispense with the old at our own peril. We will be judged, sometimes unfairly, on how skillfully we balance the two. And yes, some of us make a bit of a hobby out of doing that judging. (Don't hate us because we're grammatical!) Historical perspective and modern realities cannot be ignored, but they don't mean all sentences are created equal. Disputed usages may be fine, but some of us are shooting for more than just fine.

In these pages, I'll explore what I care about (and hope you do, too), what I don't care about (and think you shouldn't either) and why. Why do I care so much? Am I so right while so many are so wrong, or am I just suffering from a personality disorder? Maybe I'm just a big, fat elitist. Or maybe I have more in common with the learned spoilsports than it appears.

Whatever those answers turn out to be, when it comes to using words and punctuation marks and capital letters in an informed and careful way, I *could* care less. Is that so wrong? I don't think so. You couldn't agree more? I couldn't be happier!

My Web site is The Slot (www.theslot.com), named for the position of the chief on the horseshoe-shaped newspaper copy desks of old, and I offer usage commentary in doses of 140 characters or less as @TheSlot on Twitter. You'll find a sampling of my tweets in the gray boxes at the top of right-hand pages.

PART ONE

# In Theory

# 1.

# Caring, More or Less

ARE PEOPLE JUST CARELESS?

*A turd*
*becomes a fossil.*

Now, don't get me wrong. *Could care less* is hardly the most pressing issue in modern English usage, or even my biggest pet peeve. Yes, I *could* care less, but I could also care *more*. (I don't like to brag, but I'd say my level of caring is precisely where it should be.) Still, the phrase is a handy litmus test: so basic, and yet people get so acidic about it.

In this corner are the sticklers, the *prescriptivists*. We are the copy editors, English teachers, usage mavens, armchair grammarians and others who revel in dos and don'ts and in our own opinions, who *prescribe* usage. If you're a stickler, you deplore the idea of using *could care less* to mean *couldn't care less*. What could be more obvious than a preference for saying what you mean over saying the exact opposite? "One of the surest ways to show the world that you are a slipshod stylist," writes Charles Harrington Elster in *The Accidents of Style*, "is to write *I could care less* instead of *I couldn't care less*."

In the other corner are the *descriptivists* who pooh-pooh our fun. Spoilsports. They emphasize that the language is what its speakers make it, and that speakers handle that responsibility just fine. They see the glass as half full, while we're arguing over whether *half full* gets a hyphen. They are the linguists and those who have fallen under the linguists' spell, the laissez-faire realists who take their pleasure in stepping back, hands off, and *describing* how language is used. Their only strong opinions are about those who have strong opinions. Jan Freeman, a self-described "recovering nitpicker" and former language columnist at the *Boston Globe,* calls the *could care less* issue "one of the great language peeves of our time." Surveying a vast field of sticklers who "continue to insist that 'I could care less' really must mean 'I care to some extent,'" she retorts: "But it doesn't; it never has; it never will."

Sifting through the claims and counterclaims about how *couldn't care less* mutated into its literal opposite and just how wrong or perfectly fine that is, I find it telling just how often people feel the need to explain the literal meanings of the competing versions. *Couldn't care less* is oblique. It's an intentional double negative, as opposed to the ain't-got-none kind, so processing the meaning requires a couple of seconds' thought. (Who has time for *that?*) Complicating matters further if you're the literal type, the original expression is hyperbolic. Think about it: When someone says "I couldn't care less" (or says "I could care less" and *means* "I couldn't care less"), how often is the subject at hand truly the one thing that person cares least about in the whole wide world? You might say you couldn't care less about the color of the dress that the first lady wore to the State of the Union address, but you'd be exaggerating for effect. I could no doubt come up with plenty of things you care even less about—maybe the color of the garment worn by a Bulgarian farm wife you've never heard of before and will never hear of again. Conversely and sort of perversely, saying "I could care less" would virtually always be literally true, even if it's the opposite of what you meant.

---

### A REEL MESS

*"Fasten your seat belts. It's going to be a bumpy ride."*

What was bumpy in *All About Eve* was the night, not the ride.

---

## Decades of Disparagement

*Could care less* was apparently born in the 1950s. Yes, another baby boomer! Ben Zimmer, the prominent language writer and former dictionary editor, found it in the *Washington Post* in 1955. "Couldn't care less," interestingly, isn't much older—Zimmer traces it to 1944. Jan Freeman dug up the earliest known complaint about the variant, a 1960 letter to Ann Landers. Ann sided with the complainer, to the extent that she cared about the issue (yes, she said that extent couldn't have been less). For the next few decades, those who cared enough to write about the dispute agreed with her verdict, if not her lack of ardor. In his *Miss Thistlebottom's Hobgoblins* (1971), Theodore M. Bernstein of the *New York Times* bemoaned the "senseless abbreviated form" but observed that it "has not really taken hold." Bernstein opined that people shorten the expression "because their hearing is defective or because they are in an inordinate hurry, or merely because they think it cute."

Another Timesman, William Safire, was ready to write an obituary for "could care less" less than a decade later. "Happily," he said in an On Language column included in a 1980 anthology, the expression "seems to be petering out," having peaked in 1973. He pointed to the *Harper Dictionary of Contemporary Usage*, which called it "an ignorant debasement of the language." (In the same entry, Freeman points out, Isaac Asimov said, "I don't know people stupid enough to say this." Ah, those were the days.) Safire concluded: "Farewell, 'could care less'! You symbolized the exaltation of slovenliness, the demeaning of meaning, and were used by those who couldn't care less about confusing those who care about the use of words to make sense." The eulogy was premature, and writing in the *Times* in 1983, Safire observed that "the short form is understood and the long form would be regarded as the sort of thing a visiting Martian might say." But he wasn't giving up; in the same column, he spun around to venturing that the phrase would atrophy from disuse.

If only. Safire and Bernstein are no longer with us, but *could care less* lives on, in speech and writing, in sticklers' peeves and spoilsports' rationalizations. The battle lines are predictable. The not-shy prescriptivist Robert Hartwell Fiske, in his *Dictionary of Unendurable English*, says, "However it is meant, whatever the speaker's intention and inflection, the phrase *could care less* means just the opposite of the one it is so often misused for." In his *Common Errors in English Usage*, Paul Brians says, "People who misuse this phrase are just being careless."

Bryan A. Garner, in his authoritative *Garner's Modern American Usage*, disapproves of the expression but puts it at Stage 3 on his Language-Change Index, halfway between "rejected" and "fully accepted." That means it's "commonplace even among many well-educated people but is still avoided in careful usage."

In *Word Court*, Barbara Wallraff defends the usage as an informal though illogical idiom but says it's "not considered appropriate for formal speech or writing."

*Webster's New World Guide to Current American Usage* summarizes the history and concludes that "the efforts of conservative

English-speakers are not likely to be successful, for *could care less* seems too well established to be dislodged now."

On the let-it-be side of the spectrum, Jan Freeman has plenty of company. John E. McIntyre of the *Baltimore Sun*, like Freeman a self-styled reformed stickler, says that *could care less* is an idiom and that idioms are inherently illogical. "You may not care for *could care less*, but I could care less about your objections," he writes on his blog. "And frankly, apart from the tiny company of peevers, no one else gives a tinker's damn either." Freeman, writing in the *Boston Globe*, elaborates on the idiom notion: "So let's stash the phrase in the 'idioms' bin, along with 'head over heels' and 'have your cake and eat it too,' and forget about it. Truly, there is nothing more to say."

### A DICTIONARY DISSENT

*Accouterments, accoutrements*

Maybe I'm just a pretentious person who hangs out with other pretentious people, but I've never heard someone say "a cooter mint"—it's always the French pronunciation, and I think the word should get the French spelling. The *Merriam-Webster* and *American Heritage* dictionaries agree, leaving *Webster's New World*—which is the basis for most U.S. newspapers' style decisions—as the outlier.

Meanwhile, I'll be calling an envelope an *EN-velope* and calling a niche a *nitch* and calling the *AHN-velope* and *neeche* people pretentious, so maybe consistency isn't my forte. (That's *fort*, not *for-TAY*.)

## The Logic of Sarcasm

I'm not so sure there's nothing more to say, and not only because I promised the publisher 60,000 to 70,000 words here. I used to think *have your cake and eat it too* was nonsensically redundant, until I realized that the *have* means "possess," not "eat." Other sticklers point out that *eat your cake and have it too* would be more logical. That might be a good edit, if we were allowed to edit old sayings, but I see no illogic in the standard word order. *Head over heels* is illogical, but it's truly an idiom, in the sense that a logical version does not exist. When you open the catalogue to shop for an expression, *heels over head* is not there. It may have once been extant, but now it's extinct. The logical *I couldn't care less*, on the other hand, is *right there in front of you*. It's readily available. Not only that: Unlike some sticklerisms, it costs no more than the illogical alternative. When we insufferable pedants choose *careering down the street* rather than *careening down the street*, or *stamping ground* over *stomping ground*, or even *running the gantlet* rather than *running the gauntlet*, we pay a price. Our words might be received with raised eyebrows or blank stares or "What are you talking about?" or even "That's not the right word!" The variants are well on their way to eclipsing the originals. But *couldn't care less* is alive and well. It's an unremarkable expression. There's an expression for such expressions, and that expression is "That's the expression." Does a failed attempt to reach for another expression even count as an idiom?

Some defenders of *could care less* bravely venture out of the immunity-from-making-sense zone and argue that the expression is sarcastic, or at least ironic. McIntyre covers both bases, observing in another post that "when I ask if anyone has ever taken 'I could care less' in any sense other than the ironic, no volunteer has stepped forward." In the traditional sarcasm model, I suppose, one would be sneering "I could care less" with the same tone used for "I just *love* looking at pictures from your vacation in Gary, Indiana." Or—different tone, same result—the expression is shorthand, a clipped way of saying "I *could* care less, but I don't." A modern variant offers myriad choices for the colorfully profane: "I could *give* a [bleep]." (Imagine Rhett Butler's line updated to "My dear, I could *give* a damn.")

These observers, in many cases, see the sarcasm as obvious. In his book *The Language Instinct*, psychologist Steven Pinker chastises people like me who fail to hear this in the spoken form, who have a "tin ear for prosody (stress and intonation) and an obliviousness to the principles of discourse and rhetoric." Contending that the stress in *I could care less* is on the *care*, whereas in the original expression it's on the *couldn't*, he cites this as an illustration that the newer version "is not illogical, it's *sarcastic*." He continues: "The point of sarcasm is that by making an assertion that is manifestly false or accompanied by ostentatiously mannered intonation, one deliberately implies its opposite. A good paraphrase is, 'Oh yeah, as if there was something in the world that I care less about.'" (He further attributes the "could care less" usage to "today's youth" and "teenagers," which strikes me as even stranger than the sarcasm assertion. Plenty of my usage peeves are generational, but this isn't one of them.)

Michael Quinion, on his World Wide Words site, endorses the Pinker theory and says, "The intent is obviously sarcastic—the speaker is really saying, "As if there was something in the world that I care less about.'" He goes on to speculate: "There's a close link between the stress pattern of *I could care less* and the kind that appears in certain sarcastic or self-deprecatory phrases that are associated with the Yiddish heritage and (especially) New York Jewish speech. Perhaps the best known is *I should be so lucky!*, in which the real sense is often 'I have no hope of being so lucky,' a closely similar stress pattern with the same sarcastic inversion of meaning."

To me, the intonation is flat, not sarcastic—and, though my Yiddish is pretty rusty, most certainly not Jackie Mason-sarcastic. Garner writes: "Although some apologists argue that *could care less* is meant to be sarcastic and not to be taken literally, a more plausible explanation is that the *-n't* of *couldn't* has been garbled in sloppy speech and sloppy writing." (*Apologists. Sloppy speech and sloppy writing.* I like Garner.) He quotes a linguist named Atcheson L. Hench, who wrote in 1973: "A listener has not heard the whole phrase; he has heard a slurred form. *Couldn't care* has two dental stops practically together, *dnt*. This is heard only as *d* and slurring results. The outcome is *I c'd care less*."

On Language Log, Mark Liberman vigorously defends *could care less* as "a well-accepted colloquial expression in contemporary American English" but also disputes the sarcasm idea. "It's a *reeaallly* great hypothesis—I just *looovvve* it," Liberman says of Pinker's passage. (No, he doesn't. I made that last quote up.) Liberman does, however, sort of imply that Pinker has a tin ear for prosody (stress and intonation). He questions (a) whether Pinker is accurately capturing the way people say those phrases and (b) whether, even if he's right about the way people talk, sarcasm can necessarily be inferred from it. I'm not a linguist—I don't have access to Mark Liberman's fancy voice-o-meters or even, presumably, his ear for prosody (stress and intonation)—but that's in line with what I've felt since I first heard the same argument. I don't think I've ever heard "I could care less" said with a sarcastic tone. And besides, can you be sarcastic on behalf of a third party? I've certainly never heard "*He* could care less" or "*She* could care less" or "*They* could care less" said with a sarcastic tone. And it's not easy to write with sarcastic stress and intonation, at least not without italics or capital letters or boldface. Liberman also dismisses the notion that the usage is a youth phenomenon. (Hey, we're getting along pretty well for two people who disagree about the main point here.)

Liberman's analysis of what is happening, given that sarcasm *isn't* happening, is fascinating and complicated, full of cool new terms (*negation by association, the minimal object, negative polarity item, the contractual associate of the negation*). It's all rather inside-baseball, but I'm sort of the linguistics equivalent of that Jonah Hill character in *Moneyball*, and so I think I understand it pretty well. I think the bottom line is pretty close to the one Garner cites. People say "could care less" not out of an intentional desire to be ironic or sarcastic, but rather because the original phrase branched off and formed a mutation in which, for whatever reason, the *n't/not* was lost.

Arnold Zwicky, another of my favorite Language Loggers, weighs in on the Liberman-Pinker prosody argument by pointing out that the reason people use *could care less* today need not be the same reason it came about in the first place. Today it's "an idiom with negative import that happens to contain no standard negative marker," perhaps sometimes used with sarcasm, Zwicky says, and while Liberman's non-sarcasm cosmology seems valid, it need not be the whole story. Sarcasm may have played a role as well, Zwicky allows.

## Vulgarity, Anyone?

In another elaborate attempt to explain all this, in a 2004 Language Log post, Stanford linguistics professor Christopher Potts lists *couldn't care less* among "a handful of English constructions in which, quite surprisingly, one can add or remove a negation without change of meaning." I'll give him credit for the surprise, but I don't see his other examples as analogous. *Could care less*, he notes, "comes in for a hard time from some prescriptivists," whereas "the others haven't caused a stir, as far as I know." All with good reason, I say. The first of his five examples, one that he credits partially to Paul Postal of New York University, is the *vulgar minimizer*: "Eddie knows squat [or jack or beans or diddley] about phrenology" means the same thing as "Eddie doesn't know squat about phrenology." But that one is easy enough to explain. The vulgarity in question is by definition worthless, and the less-than-worthless construction is a perfectly common and logical intensifier. If I like Chevys, I might say your Ford is [bleep]. If I'm feeling particularly pro-GM that day, I might say your Ford *isn't* [bleep]. It doesn't even rise to the level of [bleep].

Potts adds his own examples to the one Postal discussed:

* *"That'll teach you not to tease the alligators"* and *"That'll teach you to tease the alligators."*

* *"I wonder whether we can't find some time to shoot pool this evening"* and *"I wonder whether we can find some time to shoot pool this evening."*

* *"You shouldn't play with the alligators, I don't think"* and *"You shouldn't play with the alligators, I think."*

* *"I couldn't care less about monster trucks"* and *"I could care less about monster trucks."*

I probably shouldn't be poking the linguistic alligators, but here goes:

* Learning not to tease the alligators and learning to tease the alligators are two sides of the same coin, and so the sarcastic "That'll teach you to tease the alligators" works as a wry twist on the straightforward statement "That'll teach you not to tease the alligators." Similarly, we ask

"How do you like that?" both as a straightforward question about a positive situation and as an ironic comment about a negative situation.

* To wonder about the possibility of billiards-related activity is, likewise, a binary equation; by definition, you are also wondering about the alternative, which is an absence of billiards-related activity. Expressing either implies the other. The spoilsports love to mock the sticklers' obsession with taking double negatives literally, but I have to point out that the "could(n't) care less" analogue of the pool-playing example would look more like the difference between "I can't play pool with you today" ("Sorry. Some other time?") and "I can't not play pool with you today" ("I can't wait!").

* The "I don't think" thing is a bit of a red herring, more a speech tic than a convention of usage. You wouldn't be likely to see it in writing. To the extent that it merits analysis, though, I think the "I don't think" version is quite a bit different from the "I think" version. The latter is a straightforward expression, whereas the former is a repetition for emphasis, a way of saying "You shouldn't play with the alligators. No, I don't think you should."

* To declare which side of a line one's degree of caring falls on is not binary in the same way as the alligator-teasing and pool-playing examples. A true parallel in the billiards case would be something like "Do I care about monster trucks?" The gator case is what sarcasm really looks like, as opposed to the fake sarcasm the apologists see in "I could care less." The parallel would be a simple "I really care," with its meaning reversible through sarcastic intonation.

The vulgar minimizer—or minimal scatological object (MSO), to use Liberman's term—is a more compelling explanation, though I still think it's flawed. "I could give a [bleep]" is pretty darn close to the idea of a sarcastic "I could care less," but the sarcasm prosody (stress and intonation) in the profane example is clear. There's an implied "like" (that's "as if" to you sticklers). On top of that, consider the takes-a-second-to-sort-out complexity and built-in hyperbole of "I couldn't care less." If people have at least a little trouble figuring out what the original phrase literally means in the first place, is a sarcastic inversion of it really going to roll off the tongue?

Here's how sarcasm works: You take an unambiguous phrase or sentence and say it in a tone, in a situation, or with a gesture or facial expression that makes it clear you mean the opposite. Your rival is marrying your ex, for whom you still have feelings? You might say, "I *couldn't* be *hap*pier." The idea that, sometime in the 1950s, people chose to take the hyperbolic double negative "I couldn't care less" and express sarcasm by inventing a regular old singular-negative version, expecting it to be understood as sarcastic and therefore equivalent in meaning to the double negative, seems more than a little dubious. It's a rather sophisticated bit of wordplay jujitsu. (How long would it take you to figure out what I meant, let alone whether I was being sarcastic, if I said, "I couldn't be any less happy"?) And even if that story were true of the *birth* of "I could care less," it would be a piss-poor attempt at sarcasm today to take an expression that nobody's sure about in the first place and reverse it into something that to most people means the exact same thing and expect them to comprehend both the reversal and the sarcasm.

However the contrary-to-logic meaning of the expression got frozen in place, it seems clear to me that contemporary speakers are just unthinkingly pulling it off the word shelf, not using it with direct sarcastic intent.

Speaking of sarcasm rolling off the tongue (or not), consider the following examples. Here's one from the late *Columbia Journalism Review* language columnist Evan Jenkins, in his book *That or Which, and Why*:

The article said the lawyer representing a murder victim's family made it clear that the family wasn't interested in cooperating with the media horde, "that the family could care less about exclusives." But if those people could care less, they do care some, and that's not at all what the writer meant.

Jenkins's analysis might strike the spoilsports as rote and naive, but please note that he's talking about *a news article*. The writer was simply trying to make a straightforward point, not trying to be ironic or sarcastic, as some of the apologists would have us believe all users of the expression are doing.

And looky here, in a *New York Times* story about rooms without a view:

"It will be the baby's room until he grows up," Ms. O'Connor said, "and babies could care less about views."

That's one sarcastic baby. (Call Child Protective Services!) While not recognizing the written form as evidence against the sarcasm theory, Quinion (he of the Yiddish corollary) concludes: "And because it is hard to be sarcastic in writing, it loses its force when put on paper and just ends up looking stupid. In such cases, the older form, while still rather colloquial, at least will communicate your meaning—at least to those who really could care less."

## If You Don't Know, You Can't Care

Setting aside the origins of *could care less*, let's say there are three main categories of English speakers with regard to the phrase: those who know there's a mismatch between the words and the meaning and who care, those who know but don't care, and those who haven't a clue.

[ENTER: FRANK GORSHIN]
*Riddle me this, Batman: When is a common expression, understood by all, an error?*

[ENTER: ADAM WEST, TRAILED BY BURT WARD]
*When it's an attempt to reach for a different expression.*

At Language Log, Geoffrey K. Pullum addresses the central argument between people like him and people more or less like me in scholarly fashion (and by that I mean Batman is barely mentioned at all) in an essay titled "'Everything Is Correct' Versus 'Nothing Is Relevant.'" In explaining that people like me are mistaken if they think people like him never see a usage as wrong, he writes, "Speakers will sometimes speak or write in a way that exhibits errors (errors that they themselves would agree, if asked later, were just slip-ups)."

I think *could care less* is precisely that kind of error. *Couldn't care less* isn't rocket science, but it's sufficiently complex that a speaker who has a life would have to stop and think a second to untangle what exactly that statement is saying about caring. And a lot of such speakers don't bother. They say "could care less" because they've heard it all their lives and they are parrots. (That might be a little harsh, but let's just say they're closer to being parrots than they are to being semanticists.) The sarcasm explanation would be a great one, if it were true. I come from a long line of sarcastic people, and I know sarcasm and irony and ironic shorthand when I hear it. "Like I care" and "I could give a $%^@&" (and especially "I could give a *$*!!!#") *sound* sarcastic. "I could care less" sounds like "I couldn't care less," and with good reason: The latter is what people are thinking while they're saying the former.

So it's not that we sticklers are accusing the care-less crowd of sitting down with freshly sharpened Dixon Ticonderoga No. 2 pencils and some scratch paper and trying their best but failing to solve the logic of not caring less. We're simply saying that *care-less*-ness is carelessness. An expression that began as a turd fossilized into a little rock, and those little rocks are everywhere and, boy, are they handy. A lot of people reach for those stones without thinking about what they used to be, and that, no doubt, includes notables from Kurt Vonnegut to Khloe Kardashian. We sticklers, on the other hand, like a little thinking with our speaking. Sticklers are squeamish and have long memories and hold grudges, but normal people are no longer smelling a turd.

Some people who speak of caring less have internalized this "sarcasm" nonsense, but most would agree, if made aware, that they *couldn't* care less. To exclude *could care less* from the category of "if only they knew" is to simultaneously underestimate the degree to which people would like to choose their words carefully and overestimate the degree to which people devote any effort to doing so.

## Follow Your Nose

Still, whether or not the linguistic spoilsports would agree with me that *care-less*-ness passes the Pullum test, I suppose I'm agreeing with them that, in a sense, the four words have hardened into a single unit that means the opposite of its original components. Where we appear to differ is on how tainted it is by its origins, how much the whiff of the turd lingers.

*Merriam-Webster's Dictionary of English Usage* (1994), which is widely seen as permissive when it comes to the nonstandard, is pretty sober on this one:

> The reason why the negative particle was lost without changing the meaning of the phrase has been the subject of much speculation, most of it not very convincing. No one seems to have advanced the simple idea that the rhythm of the phrase may be better for purposes of emphatic sarcasm with *could care less*, which would have its main stress on *care*, than with *couldn't care less*, where the stress would be more nearly equal on *could* and *care*. You, however, may not find this argument very convincing either.

Its conclusion is in line with the one reached by Wallraff and Quinion:

> This is what our present evidence suggests: while *could care less* may be superior in speech for purposes of sarcasm, it is hard to be obviously sarcastic in print. This may explain why most writers, faced with putting the words on paper, choose the clearer *couldn't care less*.

Mignon Fogarty, advice-centric as always in her Grammar Girl cape, puts it pretty simply: "Stick with *couldn't care less* if you don't want to irritate people."

## A BUREAUCRATIC BUNGLE

### VA

It stopped being the Veterans Administration in 1989, when the agency became the Cabinet-level Department of Veterans Affairs. Decades later, however, people haven't gotten out of the "Veterans Administration" habit. Watch out for that. And there's an additional complication. Because, conversationally, it was *the* Veterans Administration, it was appropriate to call that agency "the VA." The abbreviation lives on, but the *the* is now an anachronism. It's not "the Veterans Affairs," so the initials should be used without the definite article: "She works for VA."

# A Coin Toss?

In the politics of language as in the politics of politics, the sides in a debate sometimes give no ground in the face of a furious attack, even when such a position is unreasonable. I'll be charitable and guess that's what's going on here: The spoilsports, in their backlash against half a century's worth of anti-*could care less* peeving, only *seem* to be maintaining that there is not a milligram's worth of reason to tip the scale in favor of *couldn't care less*. They couldn't possibly consider the matter a coin-toss proposition, could they?

I guess they're saying we're being churlish when we look down on people for using *could care less*. (I'm half churlish, on my mother's side.) Well, people do what they do, and other people think what they think, and I don't see why language should be different from the rest of life. If you wear sweatpants in public, I might think you're a slob. If you make a habit of parroting illogical expressions, I might think you're on the slow side, or at least not much of a critical thinker. (If you flash your Official Linguist badge, I'll let you off, like a patrol officer deferring to a speeding detective who flips on the siren and sticks one of those "gumball" lights on the roof of his unmarked car.)

Training a microscope on that peeve was fun (if you bought this book because it's *your* peeve, I hope you're getting your money's worth), but the analysis isn't especially important. The important thing—and the linguists will agree with me on this—is that you get to take such analysis for what it's worth. Even if I'm full of squat, if "could care less" is actually the greatest thing an English speaker could possibly say, I'm free to avoid it in my own writing, fix it in copy that I'm editing and ban it from any publication at which I'm the boss. And even if the linguists are full of squat and it's a substandard usage, you're free to go around saying it to every person you meet. See how much I care.

# 2.

# Literally, Literally

## THE THING WITH ANTLERS

*What do we want? Hyperbole!*
*When do we want it? Yesterday!*

**I**f *could care less* is a "caution" sign on the stickler highway ("Whoa, slow down—does this guy know what he's saying?"), the use of *literally* to mean "not literally" is a red light. Figuratively, of course. Tell a stickler you're literally dying of thirst and he'll slam on the brakes (figuratively, unless he's driving you somewhere). His head won't literally explode, but he might literally stammer as he tries to form a cutting (figuratively) retort about administering fluids intravenously. You make yourself an easy target when you, with an entire language at your disposal, choose the term for "No, really, seriously, I'm not kidding—this is true" to call special attention to the fact that what you're saying is not, in fact, true.

We sticklers are seldom as unambiguously right about these things as we think we are, and this is literally no exception. The not-literally *literally* is well entrenched: Ben Zimmer has found examples as far back as the 1760s. Another language blogger, Stan Carey, cites non-literal (albeit literary) references by such notables as Louisa

May Alcott, Charles Dickens, F. Scott Fitzgerald, Thomas Hardy, James Joyce, Vladimir Nabokov and William Makepeace Thackeray.

Zimmer and others point to similar words that don't seem to bother people when they're used to emphasize figurative statements—*really, truly, very, totally, completely.* And there are other examples of words that exist as their own opposites. John McIntyre points to the verbs *cleave, dust* and *sanction.* As with those examples, he observes, the intended meaning of *literally* is virtually always clear.

Finally, I suppose it is fair to ask whether we sticklers are trying to ban hyperbole. (Perhaps I shouldn't be going around saying I have a gazillion objections to the non-literal *literally.*) In a typically eloquent defense, Geoff Nunberg (virtually all linguists are named Geoff) writes:

> In the end, this is an eternal story of original sin and redemption. It's natural enough for us to use *literally* in a loose way to "affirm the truth of an exaggeration," as Bierce put it. If "I'm starving" is hyperbole, then "I'm literally starving" is simply more so. And when you think about it, the critics' objection to that use of *literally* is rather odd—it amounts to saying that *literally* is the only word in the language that can never be used in a figurative way.

Yes. Yes! That *is* what I'm saying! *Precisely! Ding! Ding! Ding!*
*Literally* is a "safeword." (There I go again with my S&M allusions.) Say you're my dominatrix. I don't want you to stop whipping me no matter how many times I say "Stop! Stop! No, really, stop!"—it would spoil my fun—and so we agree that I need to say something else, a code, if I truly want you to stop. Maybe "top hat." Without such a safeword back in the non-pervert world, how could we make it clear we mean *literally* literally? If *literally* can be figurative, why can't "literally, not figuratively" also be figurative? If you

say, "No, really, I do mean this literally, not figuratively, in this case—please, for the love of God, believe me this time," I might just think you're being *super-duper*-hyperbolic. I might be even *less* inclined to take you literally.

Instead of trying to decide how far to escalate this *literal* arms race, let's just stipulate that *literally* is our safeword. It's our top hat. (I see that Paul Parry, a writer and comedian who calls himself the Literally Tsar and blogs about non-literal examples at Parryphernalia.com, also uses the safeword analogy.)

## A BUREAUCRATIC BUNGLE

### *CBP*

The federal agency is Customs and Border Protection, not Customs and Border *Patrol*. (The Border Patrol is part of CBP.)

# And Now for Something Completely Different

There's another option, if prop comedy is more your style. Like "top hat," it involves headgear. There's a Monty Python sketch in which Graham Chapman is Biggles, the children's-book adventure hero, trying to dictate a letter and converse with his secretary at the same time. (Note to youngsters: *Secretary* is what we used to call administrative assistants. *Dictation* was one of their duties. Instead of just typing their own damn letters, businessmen would call their "girls" and say the words aloud, and the secretaries would put paper in something called a *typewriter* and crank out the letters.)

When Biggles's secretary keeps mistaking his banter for his dictation, the great man produces a set of antlers. "When I've got these antlers on, I am dictating," he says. "And when I take them off," he continues, taking the antlers off to demonstrate, "I am not dictating." ("I am not dictating," the secretary then dutifully types.)

Let's put away the antlers and get back to our regularly scheduled programming. I think it's safe to dismiss the *really, truly, very* parallel. *Very* has roots in verity, and it occasionally makes guest appearances in that role, but today its primary meaning is . . . "very." *Really* has both "truly" and "very" as well-established, non-controversial definitions. *Truly* is a little closer, but both the "genuinely" and "indeed" meanings are well established. And while the auto-antonym or contranym—*sanction* and *sanction, dust* and *dust,* et al.—is a fascinating phenomenon, the contraindicated use of *literally* is a different matter. To dust can be to sprinkle with particulate matter or to remove particulate matter; there is no "to decidedly refrain from sprinkling with particulate matter" or "to decidedly refrain from removing particulate matter" meaning. To *not* dust or *not* sanction, like to dust or to sanction, could mean two different things. *Not literally* has just one meaning. Either form of *to dust* or *to sanction* or *to cleave* or *to buckle* or *to weather* is literally true and intended as such, whereas the non-literal *literal* is quite literally not literal. Observe:

> "Sure, you can dust the granite counter with flour to roll out your dough. But you'll need to dust it afterward."
> "Ha! That's a good one. And what's another word for *synonym?*"

> "The United Nations does not sanction genocide. It is likely to sanction that dictator."
> "You know what's also funny? Oxymorons. Jumbo shrimp! Military intelligence!"

"When I said literally, I didn't mean literally."

"Huh? Then why did you say it? Were you trying to lie to me, or are you just stupid?"

## The Apologists' Asterisks

So we're back to the hyperbole explanation. (I told you that *ages* ago.) There is good hyperbole and bad hyperbole, and the distinction tends to rest on utility and taste. Anti-peevers downplay aesthetic considerations in word choice, but not so much here. So reviled is the contraindicated *literally*, in fact, that even those with anti-stickler tendencies can get worked up about it, or at least take pains to point out that, while it's fine to keep it in *your* vocabulary, it isn't part of theirs.

John McIntyre starts his defense of the usage by saying, "Let the record show that, for my part, I prefer to use *literally* in its literal sense." He adds that he would never say that its misuse "would make my head literally explode."

Ben Zimmer qualifies his defense:

Still, that doesn't mean I think non-literal *literally* is fine and dandy—I wouldn't use it myself, and when I catch others using it I occasionally cringe. Usually, I just try to enjoy the comedic potential for interpreting hyperboles literally. So when I was watching the broadcast of the thrilling Women's World Cup quarterfinals between the United States and Brazil last month, I chuckled when I heard announcer Ian Darke say of the American women's come-from-behind win, "The U.S.A.—quite literally, really—back from the dead!" (Zombie soccer!) The laughs continued in the finals, when the U.S. player Abby Wambach said of her Japanese counterpart (and former teammate) Homare Sawa, "I couldn't be prouder of Sawa than for literally putting her team on her back and carrying them to the final." Both sports commentators and athletes themselves can't seem to get enough of *literally* as an intensifier.

Stan Carey, on his Sentence First blog, refrains from judging others but makes his personal preference clear:

> Like it or not, *literally* is used to mean more than just "literally", and it has been for a very long time. Some people—I'm one of them—prefer to use it only in its narrower, more literal senses. A subset—I'm not one of these—insist on it.

Even Gabe Doyle—a linguistics student whose blog, Motivated Grammar, is subtitled "Prescriptivism Must Die!"—is down on the usage:

> Honestly—and this may shock some of you who've been operating under the misapprehension that just because I don't like prescriptivism I am unable to distinguish better usage from worse—I don't care for non-literal *literally*. I can't find any examples of me using it in writing, and if I use it in speech, I believe I do so sparingly. My primary objection is that it strikes me as a poor word for the task; if you regularly can't find a better way to intensify a statement than cheap hyperbole, you're not a very effective writer.

Jesse Sheidlower, an eminent lexicographer, writes in *Slate*:

> The one sensible criticism that can be made about the intensive use of *literally* is that it can often lead to confusing or silly-

sounding results. In this case, the answer is simple: Don't write silly-soundingly.

Robert Lane Greene, a journalist, author and language blogger, writes in the *Huffington Post*:

> Everyone has a language peeve. Mine is "literally," a great word with no close synonym. When used as a mere intensifier or to mean simply "It felt as though . . ." it has almost no kick at all. And when misused, it can be spectacular: what Lindsey Graham recently said of an American program to turn weapons-grade plutonium into reactor fuel for peaceful energy. Truly this is a good thing, but Graham probably shouldn't have said that "the United States is literally taking nuclear swords and turning them into plowshares." My first thought was that it was pretty sweet that DARPA had finally invented nuclear swords. My second was, "But who wants a nuclear plowshare? Would you eat vegetables out of a field plowed with one?"
>
> So I'd like to keep "literally" meaning "not figuratively," and every time I see it used to mean "figuratively" I sigh a little sigh.

Neal Whitman is a linguist, but his blog is called Literal-Minded (hey, I've been accused of being that!). He says:

> I don't care that *very, really,* and *truly* have gone through the same semantic weakening that *literally* has undergone; I don't care that *literally* has been used non-literally for hundreds of years. I admit these facts, but darn it, I want there to be a word that signals you're not speaking figuratively, and *literally* is the best word for the job.

Whitman, in fact, adds a layer to the debate by pointing out that it's sometimes unclear which part of a sentence a *literally* refers to. When his wife said, "I went through a whole box of Kleenex—literally," he recalls, he was "just about to say, 'Wow, how did you make yourself small enough to go through it?' when I realized that the *literally* part wasn't about the *going through* idiom, but about the *whole box* part. She hadn't just used half the box, not just three quarters of it, but literally the whole box." He asks: "Does *literally* have to scope over the entire sentence that it's part of, or are we cool as long as it's highlighting some part of the sentence as the literal truth?"

## A REEL MESS

*"Houston, we've got a problem."*

If you're looking for the line from the movie *Apollo 13*, it's "Houston, we have a problem." Historically speaking, however, even the movie was wrong. What astronaut Jim Lovell actually said during the Apollo 13 mission was "Houston, we've *had* a problem."

I answer: We're cool. Not all potential ambiguity can be eliminated. And the not-literal-*literal* defenders point out that both senses of the word are coexisting peacefully, with scarcely a sign of conflict. But one Language Log reader posting in the comments section, identifying herself only as Diane, makes an excellent point about the potential for misunderstanding when *literally* is not literal:

I heartily dislike the use of literally for emphasis, because I think it causes unnecessary confusion. There are plenty of words that can be used for emphasis but there's really no other word that means "literally," in the sense of "actual." So if you use "literally" to mean actually and someone misunderstands it as simply a term of emphasis, it is hard to clarify without sounding neurotic.

To wit, a conversation I had recently:

ME: My husband's family is very large. He has literally over a hundred cousins and doesn't even know all their names.

HER: Mine, too!

ME: No, really, there's more than a hundred of them!

HER: [laughing] Oh, yeah, too many to count!

ME: [getting exasperated] No, I'm not kidding, his dad was one of 11 kids and his mom was one of 16 so there's literally more than a hundred cousins!

HER: Oh, yeah, that's a lot. I mean, we have, like, 20.

I search Twitter now and again for examples of the dreaded *literally*, and I'm pleasantly surprised to see how often it's used correctly. On the other hand, I'm depressed at how easy it is to find people writing that they literally could care less, an exacta of inexactitude that I can only conclude is part of a concerted effort to literally make stickler heads explode.

## A REEL MESS

*"Play it again, Sam."*

I used to see this misquote from *Casablanca* more often. Either people have wised up or they've forgotten the Woody Allen movie by that name—what Bogart said was simply "Play it, Sam."

# 3.

# The Trouble With Apologists

COMPLETING THE EVOLUTION ANALOGY

*Sure, language mutates, but how much
do you really like mutants?*

My wife is a weather geek. She gets excited when she hears about a tropical depression that might turn into a tropical storm that might turn into a hurricane. She watches hurricanes and roots for them to get bigger.

On the Internet message boards where she hangs out with like-minded weirdos, the uninitiated sometimes pop in to express their outrage at such a mind-set. "Homes are being destroyed! People are being killed!" they correctly point out.

And she correctly points out: Nothing she or the other hurricane aficionados do or say could change that.

When it comes to my beefs with the learned spoilsports, I guess I end up being on the wrong side of this anecdotal analogy. I complain that they revel a little too eagerly in language change, and they point out that they're merely observing phenomena that would be happening regardless of their interest. They're descriptivists, and so they describe. They like their work, and so it's understandable that all their observing and describing and cataloguing and analyzing will breed a certain enthusiasm. Prone to parody as I am, I picture them coming across a new erroneous usage and dancing in the streets in celebration. "Hooray! Some dude called a loofah a falafel, so now *falafel* means loofah!"

That doesn't really happen, of course. That would be silly. You might as well imagine the members of my tribe cheering the release of a new edition of the *AP Stylebook*. Come on—who would do *that*? Still, it's hard not to read that ardor, occupational hazard though it may be, as cheerleading. Fine, everybody uses "beg the question" to mean raise the question, but do you have to be so darn *happy* about it?

---

### A DICTIONARY DISSENT

*Workingman/workingwoman, working man/working woman*

The three major dictionaries all disagree with me here. The one-word masculine form is bad, but *workingwoman* is so breathtakingly awful, such a horrid scoop of alphabet bouillabaisse, that I figured it must have been purely a defensive maneuver to avoid accusations of sexism once the lexicographers had backed themselves into the *workingman* corner. A Google search suggests I'm wrong—the one-word forms are more common than the sensible-looking ones. (Why stop there? Why not *workingdogs?*)

---

## Natural Selection and the Mutants

A nd although loofahs are still loofahs and falafel is still falafel, the question of just how quickly the non-sticklers rush to embrace mutations as new species is at the heart of our little quibble. (The spoilsports might phrase that in terms of just how long sticklers continue to build zoos to house long-extinct animals.)

Language evolves, but the evolution analogy comes with a critter whose role the learned linguists don't seem to mention: the predator. What is natural selection, survival of the fittest, after all, without the prospect of being eaten? We are all predators when it comes to language, though there are big differences in our degree of ferocity. Even the tamest predator, the most descriptive descriptivist, will correct a toddler who calls a spoon a "fork," or acknowledge that a loofah is not a falafel. In all the debatable cases, though, while we sticklers shake our heads at people who don't bother to learn what words mean, the spoilsports nod sagely and applaud such confusion as the lifeblood of the language. Notables from William Faulkner to Dennis Rodman said *irregardless*! Change is inevitable, they say, so why resist?

The answer, of course, is that while change is inevitable, no *specific* change is inevitable. Not all mutations survive. Some that appeared inevitable a few decades ago are scarcely more common than loofah-as-falafel today. People stopped calling refrigerators "frigidaires." *Thru* and *employe* and *cigaret* and other simplified spellings that seemed like the wave of the future didn't last. People don't talk about "gifting" one another the way the sticklers feared in 1960 or so. No matter how many people drink "expresso" and eat "sherbert," smart people insist on the actual words. But many mutations do survive. Nouns become verbs, jargon becomes mainstream, foreign words become English ones, trademarks become generic, errors become accepted. Spellings even change. (You may have smiled at the idea of not correcting a toddler, but I saw a child's mutation survive when my little sister, Jennifer, first signed a school paper with the short form of her name. Here we were thinking she was Jen, but that day she became Jenn.)

## Case Studies

The verb *contact* was once a target of stickler scorn, but it passed the evolutionary test and lives peacefully today with relatively few natural enemies (unless you count the objection preserved, as if in amber, in *The Elements of Style*). Contrast that with the fate of *impact* as a verb, at least in the non-dental sense, which despite its ubiquity, despite its being used by notables from F. Scott Fitzgerald to Wink Martindale, has yet to win over the proverbial careful writers and editors. The two verbs aren't that different, but perhaps the taint of ad-speak and the ready synonym *affect* doomed *impact* to linguistic purgatory. Those are my guesses, at least, but the answer could just as easily be *just because*. The linguists might consider that reality a tad ridiculous, but they don't get to embrace some of the forces involved in natural selection and reject others. If acceptance is subject to crowdsourcing, so is opprobrium.

The *contact* debate was before my time, and *impact* is probably "skunked," as Bryan Garner would put it—the object of so much scorn that it's best avoided regardless of any merits it might have. If you're looking for some live Darwinian theater early in the second decade of the 21st century, try *flash mob*. Whether or not the *Oxford English Dictionary* dates the term to Chaucer's time, *flash mob* came into its own not long ago to denote a social-media-organized outbreak of performance art or just plain silliness. The ink wasn't yet dry on that dictionary definition when reporters in Philadelphia, no doubt parroting a cop or two who had heard the term and figured it meant something else, started using it to mean impromptu youth-gang violence. The predators failed to nip that one in the bud. (You might think you know what *phone booth* means, but if the pretty girl in magenta from the T-Mobile ads appears at an electronics-industry trade show, it just might suddenly also apply to the table she stands at.)

Sometimes, yes, I waste emotional energy on lost causes. When I hear Starbucks being called a *coffee shop*, I say, hey, wait a minute, I know it's a shop that sells coffee, but doesn't *coffee shop* already mean something else? (I've had two eggs over easy with crisp bacon and sourdough toast at enough of them.) I cringe as I watch those TV house-hunting shows and hear, over and over and over, people use *downfall* to mean *drawback*. ("I liked that place, but the fact that it didn't have granite countertops and stainless-steel appliances was a real downfall.") Sometimes those "downfalls" are "showstoppers." Yes, people think that word means "dealbreaker." Call me an authoritarian bastard trying to control the minds of the masses if you like, but I don't happen to think such beliefs should be encouraged.

## Who's Being Helpful Here?

It might be tempting to view the language liberals' approach as evidence that they are charitable to humankind while people like me are on the misanthropic side—and we don't do ourselves any favors by branding ourselves as grammar Nazis or Testy Copy Editors or the Grouchy Grammarian or, ahem, *curmudgeons*—but let's look at that hypothesis a little more closely. If a recent immigrant at the farmers' market asks me whether "two apples" or "two apple" is correct in English, I will helpfully explain what's right and what's wrong. I will not shrug and say, "You people say 'two apple,' so it's part of you people's dialect, and that's no better or worse than the dialect I was taught, in which it would be 'two apples.'" That would be patronizing, and it wouldn't be any more constructive than taking an El Marko to the poor guy's sign. I think it's safe to say that people in general like to be educated, and most don't like to be patronized. It's not only absolute beginners who seek out advice about correct usage. I look up words; I imagine you do, too. If it turns out I've been using a word incorrectly, I make a note of it and try not to make the same mistake again; I don't write a *Dear Mr. Webster* letter asking that my misapprehension be enshrined as definition No. 7.

If you tell me that notables from Sir Francis Bacon to Bobcat Goldthwait confused *imply* and *infer*, I might find that interesting. It's also interesting that we park in driveways and drive on parkways, but neither of those interesting morsels of interestingness is particularly helpful to me as I continue my quest not to sound like an idiot in the early decades of the 21st century. When I find myself ridiculed for helping others on their versions of that quest, I picture myself as a wine critic challenged for a dismissive review of one of those we-call-all-red-wine-"burgundy" burgundies that come in a jug. The imaginary angry letters go something like this:

> *You call this the wrong wine to serve, but it is you who are wrong. This wine has been produced since 1910, Julia Child served it, and it gets you plenty drunk.*

Never mind that it was entirely possible to make bad wine in 1910, as it was to make bad word choices in 1760. Is there really a statute of limitations on such things? (Perhaps there's a *statue* of limitations. People have been saying that for a long time, too.)

## Time, Place, Context

In the picky-about-the-language biz, we tend to fall back on platitudes about "effective communication," but that's not really the issue, even if it is more likely to sell books to deep-pocketed customers looking to improve their business acumen. (*Supercharge Your Word Power!*) The truth is, effective communication comes in many flavors. A grunt or a blow to the head can communicate just as effectively as a well-crafted sentence. "I ain't got none" gets across the same point as "I don't have any." I imagine even the most indescribably insistent descriptivist would describe the blow to the head as *wrong*, but a grunt might be enough to join the double negative in getting a promotion to one of the technical terms that the Fonzie-esque linguists use where we might use "wrong." *Nonstandard. Colloquial. Dialect. Of a different register.*

The spoilsports will protest my Fonzie comparison. They'll say they are quite willing to use the *wr-* word, just not as promiscuously as some of us. They might point out that they're fine with "I could care less" but not, say, "care I less could." They're fine with "I ain't got no" but not "I xygbiouczif got no." (Fair enough, but who's on the other side of that argument?) It's not that the language has no rules, they tell us; it's that the rules are based on what people actually do and don't do. In rare cases, the spoilsports are willing to apply *mistake* or even *error* to something more controversial than letter salad or word salad, to something that somebody in the real world might actually say. If a rapper straight outta Compton says "I is," that's grammatically correct in his dialect. But if Professor Kingsfield says "I is" after one too many glasses of sherry in the faculty lounge, that could be called a grammatical mistake.

The registers-and-dialects thing is a valid point. Standard English is not the only valid way of communicating. We're not all Thurston Howell III, nor are we all Ma and/or Pa Kettle. Different social classes and different regions mean different dialects. We don't talk to babies the way we talk to our peers, and we don't talk to our peers the way we write a term paper or a newspaper article or a book. Different situations mean different registers. Lynne Truss and the *Great Typo Hunt* dudes might get their unmentionables in a bunch about less-than-literate signage, but if I'm back at the farmers' market where I helped that nice immigrant gentleman and I'm looking to unload bushels of home-grown tomatoes, I'll bet you a Costco-size vat of mayonnaise and a dozen loaves of supermarket-brand white bread that the "right" thing to do is closer to a purple-crayon-on-cardboard "fReSH tOMAtOe'S" sign than a meticulously crafted 1,080-dpi work of high-quality ink on posterboard promising meticulously punctuated produce in a tasteful Copperplate Gothic Bold. Sometimes a less formal, less stickler-approved register is best. Sometimes the best register involves lapsing into a different dialect. It's true.

So allow me to stipulate something that really should go without saying: What we're talking about when we talk about rights and wrongs is the English used by educated people. We are talking about *standard English*, in my case standard *American* English. I don't make a habit of correcting innocent missteps in speech or e-mail or shopping lists, and so I would narrow that even further, to a subset of standard written English that could be called *standard American English in writing for publication*. (Yes, there are vigilante editors who apply that standard to speech and e-mail and shopping lists; I'll deal with those louts elsewhere.) This "correct English" critter is slippery and elusive, impossible to corner and always reinventing itself, but it's a thing. It's the thing that writers—and, to some extent, speakers—aspire to if they care enough to think about the way they write or speak. This is the arena in which we're playing. When people ask for guidance about English, we know they aren't looking for help in the proper use of hillbilly dialect or rapper dialect or Valley Girl dialect or middle-class Midwestern elementary-school-playground slang, valid as those systems of communication might be. To counter my pontification about a specific point of usage by asking "What about all those other dialects and registers?" would be like weighing in on the infield-fly rule with "Yeah, but what about football and basketball and hockey?"

### A DICTIONARY DISSENT

#### *Adviser, advisor*

I grew up internalizing the *-or* spelling, and so I was stunned to learn as I began studying journalism that the major dictionaries all prefer *-er*. I cling loosely to my *advisor* preference.

## Salsa and Solecisms

Fast-forward three decades from *Happy Days* and you might land on *Top Chef*. On one episode of that cooking-competition reality show, a contestant prepared some Mexican food that the judges found tasty. But that "cheftestant" made the fatal mistake of referring to his flour-tortilla-wrapped cylinders of chicken as *enchiladas*.

*Flour* tortillas, snapped the guest judge, Hugh Acheson, are for *burritos*! (Actually, a writer for the *Austin Chronicle* pointed out, they were more like soft tacos.) The head judge, Tom Colicchio, is a master of the terminology gotcha, and he piled on, and the contestant was eliminated for his yummy but appellationally challenged dish.

For a Tom, Colicchio would make a great Geoff. Sometimes I think the great divide between the sticklers and the spoilsports could be bridged by a simple agreement on terminology. We get in big trouble for tossing around *right* and *wrong*, *correct* and *incorrect*, and the especially dreaded *not a word*. Now, even the stickliest sticklers, the kind of people who might be tossing this book into the fireplace right now because I used "stickliest," would acknowledge that those words they call *not words*, such as *irregardless* (and *stickliest*, and *cheftestant*), occupy a different category than *xygbiouczif*, and that "care I less could" is flawed in quite a different way than "I could care less." And the spoilsports have to admit that even if those non-non-words and *could care less* and the not-literally *literally* aren't *wrong*, they're . . . *something*. Nonstandard? Colloquial? Differently dialectified? I'll let the Geoffs decide what that something is.

## As You Say, Not as I Do

Critics of a purely descriptivist approach—notably Bryan Garner in his essay "Making Peace in the Language Wars" and Joan Acocella in a *New Yorker* review of Henry Hitchings's book *The Language Wars*—have pointed out that, all their apologia for the language of the common folk aside, linguists use standard, educated written English in their books and dissertations and articles and blog posts and tweets. *J'accuse!*

Acocella's observation did not sit well with some smart people who write about language. John McIntyre: "It is a naive failure to recognize that accomplished writers understand registers of English and choose the one appropriate for their purposes. Identifying a usage does not equate to endorsing it; and even if a usage is endorsed, that does not make it compulsory." Jan Freeman: "Yes, it is possible to teach standard written English and also to question the peeves and shibboleths of the grammar Nazis; I would have expected the New Yorker to grasp that fact, but apparently I would have been wrong."

If Acocella and Garner are reading too much into the linguists' consistent use of standard written English, I guess I am, too. The point, I think, is that descriptivists are tacitly endorsing the same standards that they lambaste the prescriptivists for *explicitly* endorsing. The two sides appear to agree, for the most part, on the most effective and elegant way to express oneself, even if one side calls it just one of many equally valid registers and the other side calls it "correct English." So we're back to terminology, and I'll plead guilty to that misdemeanor. Let's put it this way, Geoffs: You know the way you write? With the clarity and the elegance and the subject-verb agreement and the standard spelling? Well, *that*. That's what I'm championing. I'm trying to encourage others to strive for such eloquence. That's all. Is that really so offensive to you? I might call "I seen" a grammatical error, but I swear I don't hang out at trailer parks so I can heckle people who say it.

It's curious that I'd have to cop to that terminology crime, though—when did the apologists become such sticklers? If *could care less* can mean "couldn't care less," why can't *correct* mean "standard"? If *literally* can mean "not literally," why can't *not a word* mean "a disputed word"? For people who are so generous about every other usage that's ever been used, linguists sure get *caliente* when it's their own enchilada that's getting cooked. Yes, when you say "I could care

45

less," I know what you mean. And when I call that "wrong," you know what I mean. A burrito by any other name would taste as spicy. With sour cream, it'd be Supreme. Is that so hard to swallow?

### A DICTIONARY DISSENT

*Bootees, booties*

I'm talking about the kind you knit for babies or slip on to avoid tracking dirt on a clean floor, not the kind you—never mind. The *bootee* spelling, preferred by *Webster's New World* and *Merriam-Webster*, struck more than one of my well-read colleagues as bizarre when I pointed it out (some thought I was referring to someone or something that has been booted), and *American Heritage* is with us in making it *bootie*. So is common usage, though the Google numbers are no doubt skewed by that other meaning.

## The Hostilities That Aren't

I'm playing along with the war genre and taking my place on the stickler side, but this book is hardly a call to arms. What some call the language wars are really more like a series of border incursions, real and perceived. A stickler's screed sounds a little too much like a moral judgment; a linguist's argument sounds a little too much like a dismissal of the very idea of editorial standards, or even the very idea of taste. Peevers peeve, but I don't think any of us deny the validity of applying social-science methodology to the way people use language. And those social scientists do their thing, but I don't think any of them deny that some writing is better than other writing. The mind-sets are so different because the missions are so different. There are best practices and there is anthropology; there are exterminators and there are entomologists.

What I'm saying, when all the Mexican food is cooked and eaten, is that people on both sides need to realize there's room at the table for both us and them. But I reserve the right to start the occasional food fight.

# 4.

# The Trouble With Me

A GRAMMAR CONFESSIONAL

*A portrait of the peever
as a young man, and beyond.*

Those of us who resist language change might as well rail against gravity, some say. Well, yeah, I do that, too. ("Some" have never seen me accidentally knock over a beer.) But as is probably clear at this point, I'm not 100 percent stickler. If there were a Kinsey scale for usage politics, I imagine I would be a 2 on the scale of 0 (traditional) to 6 (libertine). If a 2 makes somebody bisexual for Kinsey, I suppose it makes me bilingual. (I'm allowed to repurpose that term, right, Geoffs?) Not that I can really brag about my broad-mindedness. Contrary to what the spoilsports might have you believe, reputable prescriptivist pundits nowadays pretty much universally reject the hoary rules-that-aren't.

Still, my schizophrenia (if I may prove it by misappropriating a technical term) goes well beyond a healthy regard for valid arguments on both sides of an issue. "How did you get so screwed up?" you might ask. Well, oddly enough, it all began in my childhood. (It's a stylebook! It's a psychodrama! It's two, two, two mints in one!)

*Say what you mean; mean what you say. Listen to what you say; read what you write.*

I wrote that, or something like it, in a letter to the editor to my high-school newspaper in frustration over people referring to the shah of Iran as "the shaw." (As I recall, I used "Pshaw!" at one point.) I'll get to the issue of parroting word choices in writing later, but the human tendency to substitute the familiar for the unfamiliar in pronunciation has long grated on me. After the shah was out of the news, I managed to spend a decade and a half seething as sportscasters kept finding "Elijah" in the name of basketball player Hakeem Olajuwon.

Welcome to my disease.

On the application that landed me my first copy-editing job, at the University of Arizona's student newspaper, I listed "obsessive-compulsive" among my qualifications. Hearing people say "meantime" when they mean "meanwhile" or "in the meantime" shouldn't pain me so, but it does. In third grade it was the classmate reading aloud about Indians smoking pipes and exhaling "puffs of tomato smoke." During a televised tennis tournament in the 1990s it was the fans being asked to read Yevgeny Kafelnikov's surname out loud and somehow coming up with things like "Karinkadinka"—just making up syllables rather than paying attention to the letters in front of them.

## A BUREAUCRATIC BUNGLE

### *DEA*

It's the Drug Enforcement Administration, not the Drug Enforcement Agency.

# Who (Whom?) to Blame?

It's not clear how I got this way, but there are hints. Neither Mom nor Dad had gone to college, but Mom collected pronunciation goofs, and Dad was an expert speller who taught typing as part of his Air Force service in the Korean War. I was not raised by wolves, but neither was I schooled by nuns or Jesuits. Yes, that's *raised*, not *reared*, and we called kids *kids* without fear of barnyard ambiguity. My nature was picky; my nurture, a little less so. David Foster Wallace wrote of growing up in a family of *snoots*—they even invented a term for their sticklerism—but my family merely dabbled in snootery.

We didn't bother with the usual "You mean '*May* I go outside, not *can*'" routine. (The Walsh brothers preferred to stay inside anyway. All three of us would become copy editors.) We weren't lowbrow enough to say *in*-surance for in-*sur*-ance, but we weren't highbrow enough to say uh-*dress* for *ad*-dress. To this day I *lay* down, not *lie* down. (I wouldn't write it that way, but I definitely think it and say it that way.) If I'm an elitist, elitism is in sad shape.

Mom definitely has some snoot blood. I don't remember much about visiting Uncle Bill and Aunt Pat in Omaha in the early '70s, but to this day I repeat some of the tongue-in-cheek usage tips that hung on their fridge.

Avoid cliches like the plague.

Don't use no double negatives.

Beware of irregular verbs that have crope into the language.

My brothers and I would shout "lee"—*-ly*—at the TV to make adjectives into the intended adverbs. In college I was so distracted by a political-science professor's use of *which* instead of *that* for restrictive clauses that I tallied those instances with hash marks in the margins of my notebook. (Yeah, yeah, I know.)

## Sports for the Not-So-Athletic

Midway through the '70s my brother Terence and I became big boxing fans, which meant a lot of putting up with Howard Cosell. Howard liked to talk about *an* unanimous decision and *an* historic fight. Turning our attention to tennis later in the decade, all three brothers had to contend with an endless parade of football and baseball specialists hired to cover a sport they knew nothing about. Between a first serve and a second serve, when a person who's actually been to a tennis match would simply shut the hell up, one of these empty suits once felt compelled to say, "On the fault, he'll go it again."

Foreign names added to the fun. Long before Yevgeny Kafelnikov there was Guillermo Vilas. Sportscasters vaguely aware of the Spanish double-L thingie would see *Vilas* and think of Pancho Villa and ignore the double-L in *Guillermo* and come up with a classic bit of hypercorrection: Just as a goil from Brooklyn might eat ersters on the half shell, the pride of Argentina became Gully-airmo Vee-us. (Years later, Arthur Ashe and others would similarly turn Andre Agassi from AHN-dray AG-us-ee into ANN-dray AH-gus-ee.) One of the few tennis specialists on the airwaves back then, the very knowledgeable Bud Collins, complicated matters on the Vilas front by pointing out that the double-L is pronounced like *zh* or even *j* in Argentina, making the winner of the 1977 French and U.S. opens Gui-*jer*-mo Vilas. (This enraged one viewer, someone aware of Spanish but not the Argentine iteration, who wrote to one of the tennis magazines to say that Collins and his broadcast sidekick, Donald Dell, should henceforth be Bud *Co-jins* and Donald *Dejj*.)

Collins, bless his heart, goes overboard in his quest for authenticity, speaking of Martina *Navra-TEEL-ova* and *Ma-RI-a Sha-ROP-ova* long after even Navratilova and Sharapova were using anglicized pronunciations. And it was amusing/annoying to listen to all the announcers try to out-French one another in referring to the Belgian great Justine Henin as *uh-NAAAH*, sometimes reducing their attempt at *Henin* into a half-syllable followed by a cat-with-a-hairball grunt, when Henin herself would then appear on a promo to say "I'm Justine HEN-inn, and you're watching Tennis Channel."

And then there's modern cable TV. I've mentioned the *downfalls* and *showstoppers* on *House Hunters* and its ilk, but wait: There's more. On HGTV and other channels, the dangling danglers dangle all over the place. *With four daughters and three sons, will any house measure up? Once the most powerful city in Spain, its power ebbed and glory faded. Simple and not a tourist spot, the minestrone steals the show. Beleaguered and broke, his rival Joe Frazier helped him out.*

## Rules of the Road

Obsessive-compulsive might be overstating things, but clearly I have a syndrome that goes beyond an intensified sensitivity to language. Following rules is part of it, but there are rules I'm adamant about *not* following as well. *Hey, wait! Don't you see that NO RIGHT TURN ON RED sign?* One block later, my descriptivist side comes out: *Just go already! Don't you see that that NO RIGHT TURN ON RED sign is completely illogical?* I am adamant about coming to a full stop at stop signs, but then there's that one outside that one supermarket in Virginia that you'd be an idiot to pay attention to. I

see no contradiction there, or in my alternating cries of *Slow down!*
and *Speed up!* It was bad enough when I was fat and lazy and drove
everywhere, but now that I'm a bicycle commuter I have a whole
new set of neuroses. When I'm out walking or biking or driving, the
question often comes to mind: Am I the only one who understands
the concept of "two-way traffic"? (I stay to the far right even when
nobody else is around. Have to leave room, just in case. To people
walking on the left, I mutter under my breath, "Go back to Eng-
land!") Double parking? An asinine euphemism for *selfishly choosing
to block the damn road.* (If you think I'm an insufferable prig about
language, just wait till I publish my bestselling treatise on correct
behavior for motorists, cyclists, pedestrians and transit riders.)

Enforcement policy could take up a chapter or three of my book
on transportation etiquette. In all facets of life, I love order, but I
hate authority. I bemoan the slobbification of America, but I bristle
at dress codes. I want people to *choose* to look good. I want people to
*choose* to pay attention to the way they dress, drive, talk, write, live.
Paying attention is a good thing. When deli employees pay attention,
I get my sandwich "to go" by answering "For here or to go?" once
rather than four times. I ask for no mayonnaise and get no mayonnaise. When drivers pay attention, my bike and I don't get run over.
When politicians and voters pay enough attention to remember the
past, they aren't condemned to repeat it.

When it comes to usage, I'm providing the information, but
you're free to use it or ignore it. I'll reserve harsh punishment for the
double-parkers. Call me a prescriptivist if you like, but think that
word through. Sure, I'm *prescribing* this usage Rx or that, but I'm not
shoving the pill down your throat.

I'm trying my best to use my etiology for good and not evil, I promise.

## 5.

# The Joy of Snobbery, the Sting of Reality

WHERE THE BEATLES AND
BROOKS BROTHERS COME IN

*What do I want? Good grammar and good taste.
And lots of analogies, apparently.*

We are constantly making judgments and forming opinions. What would life be without them? We rate, we rank, we love, we hate, we—gasp—*peeve*. Is peeving really so awful? The usage apologists aren't shy when it comes to peeving about peevers, so I know they're not smiling blankly like Mr. Rogers at *everything*. And yet a rosy optimism about the prevalence of intelligence and good sense pervades the linguists' canon. In another Language Log defense of the idea that *could care less* is sarcastic, Eric Bakovic takes language pundit Richard Lederer to task for daring to opine that those who choose the variant form—Lederer estimates its prevalence at about 50 percent—are saying the opposite of what they mean. Bakovic:

Aside from taking into account the obvious intonational distinction between the two forms, this hypothesis has the added advantage of not insulting the intelligence of the half of the population that uses the allegedly incorrect form.

As an editor well aware of the atrocities that even professional writers commit, I wonder: Have the linguists ever *seen* unedited prose? They must have—we all do, and of course the professors among them have had to look at papers from a wide variety of students. I imagine they give some of those papers better grades than others. I imagine they consider some restaurants better than others. I imagine they get as peeved as the rest of us about bad drivers and telemarketers and the louts on planes who recline their seats into our laps.

So why would something as basic and essential as language be immune from such judgment? That's the one thing in life we have to accept unconditionally? It's OK to observe that, say, drivers constantly do stupid things regardless of their licensing or experience, but it's not OK to even think that about speakers of English? I guess I'm being churlish again, but if your premise is that humans don't do stupid things, I'm not likely to be on board with your conclusion. Humans spit and litter and pollute the air with cigarette smoke and brainless whistling. And I'm not even getting near all that murder and genocide. They write about doctors treating many "patience," about "seamen" being found inside the homicide victim's body. The say "like" seven times per sentence. Humans are often idiots. Humans are human.

### A REEL MESS

*"It's Chinatown, Jake."*

The signature line from *Chinatown* is actually "Forget it, Jake. It's Chinatown."

## Call Us Aesthetes, but We'll Also Answer to "Freaks"

For normal humans, the language is a tool. They talk. They write. No big whoop. For freaks like those of us in the stickler camp, language is something more. We read and write and talk about reading and writing and talking. We form opinions. We are *enthusiasts*. And we're more enthusiastic about some ways of writing and talking than we are about others.

In language as in fashion, gastronomy, architecture and other pursuits, there is function and there is form. This sandwich satisfies my hunger, but does it satisfy my taste buds? This house provides shelter, but do I like the design? This jacket works (it protects me from the elements and from indecent-exposure charges), but does it *work*? This sentence works (it gets my point across in an understandable way), but does it *work*? In music and the arts, form is everything. Judgments about form are matters of taste, and tastes vary widely, but they coalesce to create what can be called objective criteria of quality.

There are times when you just want a greasy cheeseburger (this would be the equivalent of linguistic *register*), but Thomas Keller's tasting menu at the French Laundry could objectively be called *better*.

## More Than Just Opinions

We know what we like and what we hate, and we know there is an objective reality greater than that. Let's stroll from the restaurant over to the record store. Even if you don't care for the Beatles, you know that, in a very real objective sense, the Beatles are greater than Fleetwood Mac. And Fleetwood Mac is greater than the Eagles, who are greater than Air Supply. And *R.E.M.* > *the Psychedelic Furs* > *Tears for Fears* > *Thompson Twins.* (If to live is to love, what fun is love without its opposite for a little contrast now and then? What's more boring than those people who say "I like *all* music"?)

So, what's wrong with treating "I don't have any" as not only different from but also *better than* "I ain't got none"? What's wrong with recognizing that, although language doesn't always work logically, a logical choice is inherently better than an equally common illogical choice? The literal "literal" *is greater than* the not-literal "literal." *I couldn't care less* > *I could care less.*

And what's wrong with a detractor of Air Supply scoffing, "That's not music"? We all know darn well that such a sentence doesn't mean the band does not use musical instruments of some sort to produce notes of some sort.

## The Naked Truth

My grand music analogy makes the point that subjective aesthetic judgments and objective standards of quality are not mutually exclusive, but lousy taste in music isn't likely to have significant real-world consequences. For an analogy that illustrates that practical concern, we need to stroll from the record store to the

## A DICTIONARY DISSENT

### *Cabdriver, cab driver*

The major dictionaries agree on the smushed form, which to me suggests the pronunciation CABD-*ruhver*. I say it's CAB-DRY-*ver* and *cab driver*, and even the onewordhappy world at large overwhelmingly agrees. Google tells me that *cab driver* is more than 18 times as common as *cabdriver*.

---

haberdasher's. Liking a crappy band isn't likely to cost you a job, but dressing sloppily—like speaking and writing sloppily—just might.

What you wear is right up there with the way you speak and write in forming the impression you present to the world. The parallels between dress and language could fill a walk-in closet. Both, obviously, whether we like it or not, tend to reflect wealth and social class. Both involve the equivalent of *register*—sometimes it's better to wear gym clothes (you need to work off those greasy cheeseburgers) or overalls (back to the farmers' market again?), but if I somehow score a reservation at the French Laundry and you're there in a Florida Gators T-shirt, I'm going to be *peeved*. Some people even practice nudism, but neither baggy sweatpants nor dangling schlongs are likely to go over well at a job interview.

Fashion, too, has its objective standards of quality: A Brooks Brothers suit would make you *better*-dressed than the gym rats or the tomato vendors or the nudie cuties. While the snobs fret over the ubiquity of wearing sweatpants and saying "could care less," the slobs bemoan the just-as-real reality that such common practices still get people judged. Again, you don't get to pick which realities get crowdsourced and which ones don't, even if you're Geoffrey G. Geofferson. If you think the conventions of standard English are arbitrary and oppressive, what does that make the convention of wearing a necktie? Can you say "sartorial shibboleth"? Fashion even has its mythology. Many think you could never wear brown shoes with a blue suit, but the real snobs say it's practically mandatory. As with some of the language rules-that-aren't, there's a dilemma: Do what you know is right, or what most think is right?

In a *Slate* article headlined "The Pajama Manifesto," Farhad Manjoo made a passionate argument against the norms of what's acceptable to wear in public. Good luck with that, Farhad, and good luck to the Geoffs on creating a utopia in which people aren't judged for how they speak. Manjoo wasn't trying to write a parody of linguistic descriptivism, but he wrote a pretty great one nonetheless. All it needed was a nudist's letter to the editor criticizing GQ for its misplaced priorities.

There are lessons in these parallels on both sides of the fence. You refuse to make subjects agree with verbs, just as you refuse to put on long pants and actual shoes, at your own risk. And you marginalize the nonconformists at your own risk. Obviously, the guy in shorts and flip-flops could be the next Bill Gates or Warren Buffett or Albert Einstein. A little less obviously, perhaps, an utter disregard for spelling and grammar could be a sign of a math savant whose right brain is so large there's no room on the left. Or maybe you're talking to a master of grammar who chooses a far different register for casual conversation and e-mail.

Still, we don't have time to look beyond the surface of everyone we meet. "You only get one chance to make a first impression" is a cliche, but cliches are cliches for a reason. It wouldn't be unreasonable for an employer to infer that prospective employees who don't care about how they look may not care about doing a good job either. With language, the inferences seem even more reasonable. Grammar, spelling and other usage issues, unlike fashion, are academic subjects. They're taught in school. If someone—at least a native English-speaking someone—didn't pay attention in English class, it could be reasonably inferred that he or she didn't pay attention in other classes either and is therefore likely to be less well educated than those who did pay attention in English class. Even if that turns out to be a faulty assumption, the lack of polished language skills alone would disqualify a person for a heck of a lot more opportunities than the lack of sartorial polish.

The informality lobby has made great strides in both dress and language. It's possible, now more than ever before, to embarrass yourself in either realm by being *too* formal, but the fact remains that it's better to be *slightly* too formal than slightly too informal. The key is keeping up with the times. In the Internet age, when your writing skill is apparent to people beyond your immediate family and your co-workers and your pen pals, it's especially important that your writing give off an aura of competence. In some cases that will mean following arbitrary conventions and ancient superstitions. We wear neckties and, at least for now, we avoid the singular *they*. To use an expression that you'd think I'd hate, but which I actually find rather profound, *it is what it is*.

# 6.

# The Trouble With Sticklers

*There's a fine line between*
*snobbery and jerkitude.*

The language-snobbery thing can get complicated, but this much is simple: Don't be a jerk.

So listen here, fellow part-time jerks: Correct usage errors when you're on the job, if that's part of your job. Share humorous errors with friends who enjoy that sort of thing (even the spoilsports enjoy that sort of thing, but they invent cute terms such as "eggcorns" to avoid using the word *wrong*). Shake your head at apostrophe abuse and unnecessary quotation marks and misspellings and malapropisms and the myriad ways speech and writing can go wrong. Buy books like this. Oops—*such as* this! Buy copies for all your friends and relatives, too.

But don't make a habit of correcting innocent errors in speech or in e-mail. Verbal tics can actually, like, be quite, like, annoying, actually, as can the absence of capitalization and punctuation and correct spelling that has become all too common in electronic messages of all sorts, but different standards apply. Unless you have a very unusual job indeed, it's not up to you to correct such things. Correcting errors in speech and e-mail is a great way to get people to stop talking to you and writing to you.

Don't send back birthday cards with red-penciled proofreading marks. Don't pull out a marker and deface signs. Enjoy the delicious ethnic food no matter how broken the English is on the restaurant's signs and menus. (Just hand me the banh mi!) Don't give sticklers a bad name.

Remember that publication style is a means to an end. It's not the same thing as correctness. And if you're looking for a fetish, you could do a lot better.

If you're tempted to think less of a publication because of an error you spotted, remember this: The fact that you spotted that one does not necessarily mean you would have spotted every other one that was caught before you looked in.

Never forget Muphry's Law. That's right, *Muphry's*. It's the principle that a complaint on the Internet about usage or spelling is likely to have at least one usage or spelling error of its own. (For instance, one person's Web rant about the use of *impact* as a verb spells *effect* as *affect*.) Corollary: There's a good chance you know less than you think you do. Keep that in mind as your "corrections" reach higher degrees of difficulty.

Oh, and have some standards. A great catch is a great catch, but if spotting an *it's* that should have been *its* causes you to break into an NFL-quality victory dance, *your a looser*.

## A DICTIONARY DISSENT

### *Catchphrase, catch phrase*

This isn't exactly a vehement dissent, but I'm with *American Heritage* in preferring *catch phrase*. *Webster's New World* and *Merriam-Webster* prefer to onewordize.

# Good Cop, Bad Cop

I have been known to print out homemade parking tickets and put them on illegally parked police cars. (I *knew* there was something I left out of the chapter about my being such a nutcase.) The point of the law, as I spell out on the tickets, is public safety; it isn't to create a two-tiered system in which some people have to obey and others do not. If my car would create a hazard in that space, Officer Friendly, so would yours, and it infuriates me that you don't understand that (or choose to ignore it).

I'm sorry to have to admit that a mind-set similar to Officer Friendly's exists with too many copy editors and armchair grammarians (*vigilante editors*, as I call them). These sticklers don't disobey the rules they foist on others, but they do enforce the so-called rules for the sake of enforcing them, without thinking about what they're doing. That, to me, is kind of jerk-y.

## Of "Grammar" and "Typos" and "Judging"

*I* *Judge You When You Use Poor Grammar* is the name of a popular Facebook group that spawned a picture book, a paperback devoted largely to photographs of mispunctuated and oddly worded signs. I have mixed feelings about such a phenomenon. I'm glad people are interested in usage, but a couple of words trouble me. *Grammar* is a red flag. Misplaced apostrophes, wacky quotation marks, deranged spellings and other stickler staples have nothing to do with grammar. The term has come to be used as synecdoche, representing grammar and all other facets of usage, and the smart people behind Grammar Girl and Grammar Monkeys have adopted it, but they stand out as exceptions. In general I'm skeptical of people who toss *grammar* around, and many of those people make themselves easy to write off by calling it "grammer." (A similar fate has befallen the word *typo*. It means typographical error, as in accidentally hitting the wrong key, but today people use it for clearly non-accidental errors of all sorts in writing, whether that writing is done by keyboard or by hand.)

The word *judge* also makes me wince. I guess I do judge, but there's judging and then there's judging. If I hear a double negative, or "ain't" used non-ironically, I'm likely to make the judgment, the observation, that the speaker is not a member of my socioeconomic group. And if I hear "shall" used non-ironically, or certain pronunciations (ro-*mance*, duh-*tails*), or even "lie down," I'll make an equal but opposite socioeconomic observation. I hear a blue-collar type in the first instance and a trust-fund type in the second, and I may or may not be inclined to like either person. But *judging*? I'm pretty sure the title was intended playfully, but I fear that too many will take it seriously.

### A REEL MESS

*"What we have here is a failure to communicate."*

Even if people avoid one common error (the line from *Cool Hand Luke* uses "we've got" rather than "we have"), they tend to mistakenly insert that "a." It was actually just "failure to communicate"—"What we've got here is failure to communicate."

## What the Spoilsports Have Taught Me

Remember when nobody said "I graduated high school" without the "from"? Have you noticed how all of a sudden people are saying "can't get untracked" when they mean "can't get on track"? How "set foot in" is suddenly becoming "step foot in"?

Well, those are all examples of the *recency illusion*, one of the many basic concepts for which I have to thank those spoilsports I've been ragging on. If you didn't know who Peter Riegert was, and then you learned, and then suddenly every movie on cable TV seemed to have Peter Riegert in the cast, that doesn't mean he invented time travel and suddenly plopped himself into 1979 movies and 1996 movies. It's more likely that awareness breeds awareness and suddenly you're attuned to something you weren't previously attuned to. Here I've been simmering of late about "untracked" and the next thing I know Charlton Heston is saying it about Arthur Ashe in a tennis broadcast—from 1975. "Graduate high school" seems like such a modernism, but there's Ernest Borgnine's character saying it in *Marty* (1955). I swear I had never heard of "stepping foot" until the

65

21st century, but the *Oxford English Dictionary* has examples from 1864 and 1880.

The linguists and I might disagree about what all this means (I say it means that—surprise!—people made mistakes in 1864, 1880, 1955 and 1975, too), but we agree on a fair number of things. My passion for language has long centered on myths and their debunking. I've never had much interest in hammering home the simple things, the difference between *its* and *it's* or *their* and *there*. Those are the boring compulsories, the word-nerd equivalent of the figure eights that skaters have to cut into the ice before moving on to the real competition. And the army of volunteers ready to pounce on such errors doesn't need my help. While some of my stickler brethren robotically recite "*Media* and *data* and *graffiti* are plural," I sneak over to the spoilsport side of the playground and talk about why that's not necessarily the case. *Host* as a verb? Of course! *Hopefully* as a sentence adverb? By all means.

As much as the conventional wisdom bores me when it's right, it offends me when it's wrong, when the CW is BS. I'll be polite and bite my tongue if I hear "heighth" or "supposably" in conversation, but I may well attack the attacker if I witness a misguided assault on someone who dares to split an infinitive or end a sentence with a preposition. People do stupid things, in language and in life, but I have an especially hard time with those who *go out of their way* to do stupid things, especially in the name of being smart. They are the *meta*-stupid, sometimes even doing harm in the name of doing good. Mangling a sentence to avoid splitting a verb. Being skeptical of doctors while believing the peddlers of "miracle" cures. Tapping on soft-drink cans to "calm down" the carbonation. Eating salad to lose weight, but ladling ranch dressing on it. Some people look at cigarette smokers and say, "Sure, you may look cool, but you're going to get cancer." I say, "Nah, you don't look cool, either."

I'll take debunk over bunk any day. I don't get too upset when the spoilsports chase me off their turf for inventing an idiosyncratic counter-rule here and there, sometimes in disagreeing with them and sometimes in agreeing with them for the wrong reason. They've tried their best to save me from some of my sillier impulses. If one of them had been looking over my shoulder, maybe I wouldn't have invented a time in which every American second-grader could expound on the comma of direct address. (A cousin to the recency illusion is the myth of a golden age of usage.) I might not have called the hyphenless *email* an "abomination" that challenges whatever faith I have in human intelligence. (There are some other things to be said about *email* that only I appear to be saying, but more on that later.)

Arnold Zwicky, who(m) we met in the chapter on *could care less*, has a nice summation of how those he calls PITS (people in the street) view "non-standard, innovative, regional, informal, etc. usages." Technically I'm not in the street—I'm up here on my soapbox, reaching literally tens of people with my Andy Rooney-meets-Sheldon Cooper attempts at wisdom—but the shoe does fit. We're the sticklers, the snobs, the snoots and now we're *the PITS*. How McEnronian! And Zwicky has us pegged:

> Many of these usages have their origins in what could broadly be labeled as "mistakes" or "errors"—via regularization, reanalysis, generalization, hypercorrection, and the like—and PITS are inclined to see them as . . . errors still, as (inadvertent) failures to attain the correct usage. This attitude towards variation leads to what I think of as the Repetition Annoyance Syndrome, or RAS: PITS are mightily annoyed when speakers or writers *keep* producing the manifestly incorrect usages, time after time. "There he goes *again*", they cry out in exasperation, as "She talked with Tom and I about it" is succeeded by "That really pleased Tom

and I" and so on, one nominative coordinate object pronoun after another, in what strikes many PITS who abhor this construction as a perverse indulgence in error.

That's a fair cop. I'll spend the rest of this book making my case for the value of the traits that G. Arnold and the other Geoffs criticize. I'll resist their resistance to resistance. I'll argue that there are questions of aesthetics and utility that readers and writers and editors are free (and even duty-bound) to decide beyond the linguists' least-common-denominator determinations of what can and cannot be called wrong. When it comes to good writing, I'd rather be OCD than LCD. I'll continue what I started in *Lapsing Into a Comma* and *The Elephants of Style*, carving out my areas of agreement and disagreement with stickler dogma.

## A DICTIONARY DISSENT

*Seviche, ceviche*

When it comes to seafood "cooked" via a citrus marinade, I say "Yes, please!" And I say *c*, not *s*, as do most menus. The *American Heritage Dictionary* agrees, but *Webster's New World* and *Merriam-Webster* list *seviche* first. Google says my version is *20 times* as common.

## Be Your Own Stylebook

But this is just one book by one man setting out his opinions for this one moment. I guarantee you'll disagree, to whatever extent. Now, there are those who call me a demigod. Come to think of it, I suppose it's possible they're saying "demagogue." But no, that can't be right—it must be "demigod." Even so, you're a fool if you vote a straight party line, anybody's straight party line, on matters of language.

If you're an editor or writer, you might use Associated Press style or Chicago style or *New York Times* style or *Wall Street Journal* style or *Washington Post* style on the job. There's a term for people like you: good employee.

If you follow that same stylebook to the letter when you're off the clock, there's a term for that, too: Stockholm syndrome.

Listen here, fellow sticklers: There is a world beyond the stylebooks, beyond Strunk and White, beyond armed and hungry pandas, beyond the latest dumb-things-people-say list on Facebook, beyond what a nun may have told you while assaulting you with a ruler, beyond your peeves and mine. And there are some good ambassadors out there. Read Geoff Nunberg and Geoffrey K. Pullum and G. Arnold Zwicky and G. Mark Liberman and the other Geoffs at Language Log (languagelog.ldc.upenn.edu—catchy, isn't it?). Read Ben Zimmer, there and elsewhere. Read recovering nitpickers Jan Freeman and John McIntyre and the like-minded people they link to (have Google send you an alert when those names crop up in the news feed). You won't agree with everything they say. (I sure don't.) You might remain a stickler. (I sure have.) But you'll be a smarter stickler.

# 7.

# More Stickler Traps

*Sometimes your heart's in the right place
but your red pencil isn't.*

I'm in the newspaper business, and in the newspaper business we use *news conference*, not *press conference*. We spell out *one* through *nine* but use numerals starting at *10*. We abbreviate the names of most states when they're used with cities, and use traditional abbreviations such as *Ala.*, not postal abbreviations such as AL. So we do. So what?

I've made the point that it's wrong to call "wrong" wrong when copy editors use the word in a workplace context to mean contrary to style, or even when word nerds use it to mean "nonstandard." But I have to admit there are those among us who really do think style rules are rules-rules. I lost a well-meaning fan not long ago when I wouldn't go along with his condemnation of using hyphens in compound modifiers based on *-ly* adverbs. Sure, it's *an easily remembered rule* that the construction makes the hyphen unnecessary (an adverb couldn't possibly go with anything but the word that follows), and indeed that's a principle that's generally accepted beyond the level of individual stylebooks, but it's not holy writ. Style rulings can turn the Labour Party into the Labor Party, the Bijou Theatre into the Bijou Theater, Yahoo! into Yahoo, NIKE into Nike and adidas into Adidas. Style variation means that Muammar Qaddafi, Moammar Gaddafi and Moammar Khadafy are the same person. A member of Kuwait's royal family might have *al-* in his name four times in one publication and zero times in another.

I can and do make impassioned arguments against postal abbreviations and decorative capitalization. I opt not to use serial commas in most cases. But those who disagree with me aren't wrong; at worst, they're misguided. And so are those who equate style with correctness. Read on for more stickler pitfalls.

---

### A REEL MESS

*"Are you feeling lucky today, punk?"*

The quote from *Dirty Harry* goes, "You've got to ask yourself one question: 'Do I feel lucky?' Well, do you, punk?"

---

## Needing a Rule for Every Occasion

It is said, possibly apocryphally, that a copy editor once asked colleagues, "What's our style, Iran or Iraq?" I've never received a question that silly, but I get some that require the same "Depends on which one you mean" answer. ("Is it 'the market fell' or 'the markets fell'?") In a foolish search for consistency, people fail to see that correctness demands inconsistency. Another, more common class of foolish-consistency question seeks to impose a single answer where two or three or half a dozen might work. These tend to be searches for just the right preposition: "Is an article *on* a topic or *about* a topic?" "Do you feel anger *at* someone or *toward* someone?" "Do you drive *by* a location or *past* it?" "Do you have a discussion *of* something, or *about* something, or *on* something?" (I get a fair number of such questions by e-mail. Some people are just dying to be told what to do.)

You'll sometimes run into an editor who has an arbitrary cutoff point at which an introductory clause gets a comma. Commas, of course, are flexible ( just look at them!), and so any attempt to impose order is silly. The same introductory clause might get a comma in one case and no comma in another depending on what follows. Observe:

"In the end, you have to follow your heart," she said.

The comma seems natural there.

"Today you might shy away, but in the end you have to follow your heart," she said.

When two sentences are fused that way, the rhythm changes. The speaker probably paused before the *but* and paused less after the introductory clauses. Even if she didn't, or if you have no way of knowing whether she did, the necessary comma in the middle of the quote makes those optional commas less advisable. There are times when commas carry meaning, but this is not one of them. Nobody is going to comb your other sentences for three-word introductory clauses and call you inconsistent for using a comma there but not here.

The comma that's customarily used to introduce quotations can likewise be discarded when it gets in the way. Don't treat it as sacred.

"When I say 'Grow?' you say 'No!'" the organizer instructed the crowd at the anti-sprawl rally.

And now about that comma before *because?* Always or never? Now, that one depends, and it carries meaning.

*He didn't buy the car, because it was very expensive.* (The car cost too much.)

*He didn't buy the car because it was very expensive.* (He may be rich and ostentatious, but he bought the car for some other reason.)

The quest for an in-all-cases rule leads some to believe that parentheses containing full sentences must always be set off from other sentences. Not true. The only rule is that periods and capitalization must be appropriate to the situation. Either of these is fine:

*The last of the buildings was demolished four years later than planned (permits were delayed).*

*The last of the buildings was demolished four years later than planned. (Permits were delayed.)*

I once worked for an editor who saw "four-dot ellipses" as inconsistent with the usual three-dot variety and decreed that all ellipses in his publication would consist of just three periods. Um, yeah. The thing is, there are no "four-dot ellipses" to begin with. Ellipses consist of three dots. Often there will be a fourth dot, but that's not part of the ellipses; it's merely a period ending the previous sentence.

So basically, under this editor, we had to pretend that sentences followed by ellipses were part of the next sentence.

The fact that you're dealing with a period has some typographical consequences. Whereas the three ellipsis dots must be joined to prevent an unwanted line break, that fourth—or rather first—dot, the period, is on its own. It should be followed by a regular old space and not attached to the ellipses. In e-mail or a similarly informal format, the ellipses can simply be typed in succession. More sophisticated presentations require two "non-breaking spaces" or "thin spaces" to hold together the three dots.

To be sure, there are some non-logic-based rules for periods and commas. If it's an unbreakable rule you want, here's the place to look. In American English, commas and periods go inside the quotes. Period. Exceptions are sometimes made in technical writing, where the convention could result in an unwanted instruction to type a period or comma as part of a computer command, and by crusaders here and there who long for the logic-based system used in British English.

## A DICTIONARY DISSENT

### *Cross hairs, crosshairs*

My own hairs are a tad cross, having less company than they used to, but the word is *crosshairs. Merriam-Webster* and the world at large agree, but *Webster's New World* and *American Heritage* stick with the weird two-word form.

## Following Rules-That-Aren't

Rules That Aren't is my schtick. I've given a presentation by that
name at several of the annual conferences of the American
Copy Editors Society. Yes, I'm a descriptivist among prescriptivists, a
spoilsport among sticklers. A schtickler. It surprises me that many
professional copy editors and amateur sticklers continue to subscribe
to certain bugaboos that are not espoused by any reputable usage
authorities. I occasionally hear from people who tell me they love my
books and who then go on about how much they hate split infini-
tives, and split verbs in general, or sentence-ending prepositions or
sentence-beginning conjunctions. All those things are fine. I'm
tired of even talking about them. Pick up *The Elephants of Style* if
you need ammunition in an argument with a misguided stickler.
Likewise the need to always write in complete sentences. The taboo
against writing in the first person (you can guess how I feel about
that). The prejudice against conjunctions, especially when '*d* means
*would* rather than *had*. The ban on the word *got*. The belief that
*fast* and *slow* can't be adverbs. That *host* is never a verb. That *gender* is strictly a grammatical term. That *over* and *under* refer strictly
to spatial relationships. That *none* must always take a singular verb.
That *different than* must always be changed to *different from*. That
*hopefully* cannot be used the same way that *happily* and *sadly* and
*fortunately* and *unfortunately* are. That *media* and *data* must always
be treated as plural. That it's a good idea to delete *that* whenever
possible.

## Misunderstanding Rules-That-Are

Some of the more legitimate rules, to the extent that any of these principles can be called rules, have a tendency to get misunderstood and overcooked and misapplied. *Impact* is frowned upon as a verb meaning "negatively affect"? Well, then, I'll avoid it as a noun, too! *Due to* doesn't work the same way as *because of*? Well, then, I'll change it every time I see it! *May* implies permission, unlike *can*? Well, then, I'll change *may* to *might* every time permission doesn't apply! You're not supposed to hyphenate compound modifiers built on *-ly* adverbs? Well, then, I'll get those hyphens out of *curly-haired girls* and *family-run businesses*!

I don't like to play favorites among my babies, but if forced to name the peeves I pet most, the subject-verb follies come to mind. Some people, armed with a firm grasp of the notion of "subject" and perhaps some rudimentary sentence-diagramming experience, see *a group of* or *a host of* or *a number of* or *a range of* or *a variety of* and raise their hands like Arnold Horshack. "*It has to be 'Group is.' 'Is'! 'Is'! Pick me, Mr. Kotter!*"

With *group*, often it is *is*. With the others, it probably isn't. Grammarians will toss around technical terms—*notional agreement*, perhaps—to explain why, but I prefer to explain by example. First, to put to rest the idea that a singular noun could possibly take a plural verb, observe:

> *A bunch of us are going to the mall.*

> *A lot of people like that beer.*

*Bunch* and *lot* are singular nouns, are they not? You wouldn't say "a bunch of us is going" or "a lot of people likes," would you? There you have it: A lot of people is mistaken about this! What you have to ask yourself is whether you're talking about the group or about the members of that group. Both will be true in most cases, but one will ring truer. A lot likes the beer? No; people like the beer. A bunch is going to the mall? Well, yes, but really we mean us—we—are going.

*Lot* in the "many" sense will never be the governing noun. The singular-vs.-plural question will always be decided by the answer to "A lot of what?" If you had a lot of sushi with the aforementioned beer, a lot of sushi *was* consumed.

Note that even a noun that's a true singular entity, not used in a collective sense, will sometimes find itself in a position where a plural hijacks the number question. *Lot* in the auction-house sense can illustrate that:

> *A lot of items from the estate is now on the block. Bidding starts at $1,000.* (The verb applies to both *lot* and *items* in a way, but clearly it must agree with *lot*.)

> *A lot of items that are dear to the family could be had for a steal.* (The items, not the lot, are being described as dear to the family.)

*Bunch* is similar to *lot*, but it has a solidly singular sense that's closely related to its "many" sense. Note how obvious the verb choice is in these two examples:

> *Spring is here early. A bunch of daffodils are blooming in the front yard.*

> *The flowers are sold by the bunch. A bunch of daffodils is $5.*

*Group* is more likely to be a close call, but it works the same way:

> *A group of doctors has issued a statement opposing the new regulation.* (Picture the American Medical Association.)

> *A group of doctors have been playing that course every Wednesday since it opened.* (Picture Dr. Hartley, Dr. Robinson and Dr. Tupperman.)

Some of the other common grouper-duper nouns clearly yield to the mass-noun-vs.-count-noun nature of what they're describing— whatever other meanings they have do not get in the way:

> *A host of problems have cropped up.*

> *A whole mess of tennis balls are in the supply closet.*

> *A wide range of painkillers have been tried, with little relief.*

A harder choice is sometimes presented by *series*:

> *A series of programs is examining the issue of immigration policy.*

> *A series of programs are examining the issue of immigration policy.*

The series of programs doing the examining is made up of programs doing the examining. I'd use *is*, but it's almost a coin toss.

> *A series of explosions _____ rocked the city in the past week.*

This one is easier: The explosions did the rocking, not the series, so make it *have*.

### A DICTIONARY DISSENT

*Flowchart, flow chart*

Webster's New World and Merriam-Webster call for *flowchart*. Owch! American Heritage is with me in the land of good sense.

## More Subject-Verb Follies

Are you one of those people who insists on correctness? No, you're not. If you're still with me, you just might be one of those people who *insist* on correctness. This is perhaps the king of the stickler traps. Get it right and you may very well be forcefully corrected by one of those self-styled sticklers who *are* dead wrong.

As with *a lot of* and *a bunch of*, a misplaced reliance on (cue Arnold Horshack) "The subject! The *subject!*" leads people astray. In this case, though, it's not that the subject is buried or embedded or unimportant; it's that a lot of people look at the wrong subject. Observe:

"Matt is one of those people who likes to gamble."
"Wait—what people?"
"People who like to gamble!"
"Oh, OK. You didn't say that. You said he's one of those people,

and then you added that he likes to gamble. You didn't say anything about those people, other than the fact that he's one of them."

"Where did you get all that? No, I said he's one of those people who likes to gamble!"

"There you go again!"

"Huh?"

The original speaker—let's call her Amy—used *likes* instead of *like* in the mistaken belief that the verb must agree with the subject *Matt*, or maybe the subject *one*. But that makes no sense, because, as the dialogue with the second speaker (let's call him me) explicitly spells out, the subject in question is *those people*. If Matt is the only one whose affinity for gambling is being discussed, then what are *those people* even doing in the sentence?

If Matt's status as just one person has to govern every question of singular vs. plural in every sentence he appears in, regardless of logic, then we have to say he's *one of the best blackjack player in the casino.*

It takes a little work to construct a situation in which "one of the" or "one of those" would be used to say something about only the person named. If, say, Mr. Ensley and Mrs. McNew were in the teachers' lounge discussing their disappointment with the seventh-grade class, and Mr. Ensley suddenly thought of one exception, he might say, "Kathy is one of the students who really knows her stuff." He could have made it more emphatic—"Kathy is the only one of the students who really knows her stuff"—but perhaps he hadn't given the subject enough thought to rule out the possibility of a second good student.

> ### A REEL MESS
>
> *"If you build it, they will come."*
>
> The *Field of Dreams* line is "If you build it, he will come."

## Demonizing the Passive Voice

The active-voice fetish is an artificial thing. Passive voice, in most cases, grates on you because somebody told you it should grate on you. (Yes, this is one point on which I am in total agreement with the learned linguists.)

Really good examples of really bad passive voice aren't easy to find in the wild. They tend to be farm-raised. Often they're not passive at all. Many people (including Strunk and White and the people who keep putting out new editions of *The Elements of Style*) see a "to be" verb or a sentence beginning with "It" and think those are signs of passive voice. The examples that truly are passive tend to be made-up atrocities that no writer would ever think of committing. Strunkwhite advises against "My first visit to Boston will always be remembered by me." Well, yes. Can't argue with that.

The one genuine example that keeps getting dragged out is "Mistakes were made," a Washington staple perhaps most famously used by Ronald Reagan. The sentence has an obvious problem, but the basic structure isn't it. In grappling with the reality of the Iran-Contra scandal, we wanted someone to take responsibility, and that passive sentence evaded responsibility. *Streets were plowed* is an identically structured sentence. It might annoy you because you were trained to be annoyed by the passive voice, but does it really have you demanding to know who did the plowing? True, the plowing of streets is a benign thing compared with the clandestine sale of weapons to bad people, but consider *Banks were robbed* or even *People were killed*. Not at all benign, but still: Is there something fundamentally wrong with reporting such a fact, assuming it's not a Reaganesque misdirection from the perpetrator himself? Is it really necessary to drag the plowers into the sentence?

*The Redskins were defeated.* Passive! Who defeated them? *The Redskins lost.* Active! And, uh, who defeated them? You could argue that *lost* is a slightly tighter, more direct way of saying *were defeated*, but you still don't know the identity of the winning team. If that's your complaint about the passive version, your quarrel isn't with the choice of voice. It's with the withholding of information. Then you have to ask yourself: Does that information even matter? Maybe yes, maybe no. Casual fans who root for the home team but don't really follow football have all the information they need. Serious fans of the home team who follow the entire league closely will want more information, but they'll appreciate learning the most important fact first. Neither the passive voice nor the undisclosed information renders those sentences flawed for either audience. Now, a hard-core NFL fan who cares not a whit about the Redskins' fate is out of luck, but that's a know-your-audience problem, not an English-usage problem.

And most writers and speakers do know their audiences. I have my problems with the school of thought that holds that the way people write is right because that's the way they write, but in this case I think you can usually trust that seemingly buried details are buried for a reason. People are eager to get to the point, and sometimes the actor isn't the point. The actor might be unknown, or unimportant, or less important than the actee, or painfully obvious.

Or maybe the passive voice just sounds better. *A bill passed by the House last month was approved by the Senate on Tuesday.* Is it really better to make it *A bill the House passed last month was approved by the Senate on Tuesday?* Or *The Senate on Tuesday approved a bill the House passed last month?* Are we really better served by *the long-term dangers deficits pose* than by *the long-term dangers posed by deficits?*

Tell you what: Go ahead and follow your avoid-the-passive policy. Good luck with that. I'm confident you'll find that unknown actors and unimportant actors are suddenly everywhere. And the learned linguists have found that those who complain the loudest about passive voice use it more often than most people. Passive voice is to the sticklers what hookers are to the Bible thumpers. Mistakes are made.

# PART TWO

# In Practice

# 8.

# The Usual Suspects, and Some Unusual Principles

ELEGANT VARIATION?

*In which I come up with
reasons for the things we do.*

E legant variation is a term coined by H.W. Fowler for the discredited notion that it's a good idea to mix things up with synonyms to avoid repetition. Half a century or so ago, in what has become the classic example, Charles Morton of the *Atlantic* seized on the use of "elongated yellow fruit" on a second reference for *banana*.

I propose a rehabilitation of the term. (Of *elegant variation*, that is, not *elongated yellow fruit*.) When two more or less equally valid terms exist and there's some distinction that some readers will recognize, however minute, and you're going to vary anyway, why *not* do it elegantly rather than just flipping a coin? Why not humor the sticklers and preserve a distinction, even a minute one, if it'll avoid distracting some and not be noticed by others? (There are valid reasons not to, of course, including *I work at a newspaper and have only 30 seconds to edit this 30-inch story.* Editing often involves triage.)

My version of elegant variation is the overriding principle of a philosophy of writing and editing that I call *tiny acts of elegance*. As I look at the fading distinctions, emerging usages and other roiling disputes that make up the picky-about-the-language biz, I apply a set of principles that I'll do my best to describe here. You've been warned: These distinctions can be tiny. But the little things add up.

**Leaving room** is a term I borrowed from judged sports such as gymnastics and figure skating. Sure, that Nellie Kim or Dianne de Leeuw routine looked good, but you have to consider whether the still-to-come Nadia Comaneci or Dorothy Hamill routines might be better, and so you *leave room* in the scoring. The same principle can be applied to word choice and punctuation. I hyphenate *white-truffle purveyors* because maybe someday the race of my truffle purveyor will be relevant to something. I don't substitute *like* for *such as* willy-nilly, because sometimes I want to refer to people, places or things *like* another but not *including* that other. I don't say I literally fell off my chair when I didn't literally fall off my chair, because someday I might literally fall off my chair. So I leave room for that.

I write *$12 million to $13 million*, not *$12 to $13 million*—maybe someday I'll be writing about amounts that *do* range from 12 dollars to 13 million dollars. I distinguish between senators from Illinois (U.S. senators) and Illinois senators (state senators). Sure, people will know what you mean based on context, but why drive down a road on which Barack Obama *went from being an Illinois senator to being an Illinois senator* if you can steer around the possibility?

**The binary bind** is an overlapping principle. In its simplest form, it's the recognition that sometimes you have to choose one option or the other; if you choose (a), you're ruling out (b). This is where the reality of being a writer or an editor differs from the reality of being a linguist: In the ivory tower, it's easy to say there's nothing wrong with either choice. In the trenches, there are concrete decisions to be made. And that feeling of liberal magnanimity you might be basking in when you let a writer get away with "staunch the bleeding" on Page B2 might fade pretty quickly when you're editing the writing of a more sticklerly type on Page B3 and you have to, in effect, declare the more technically defensible "stanch the bleeding" *wrong*. When I consider whether to allow a disputed usage in my personal stylebook (or, if I'm editing, whether to let it stand), I think about what I might be giving up in return. If I decide to refer to gantlets as gauntlets, what, then, are actual gauntlets? *Gauntlets-as-in-gloves-and-not-that-thing-you-run*? *Gauntlets-as-in-gauntlets-no-seriously-I-really-mean-it*? What if gauntlets and gantlets come up in the same book, the same article, the same sentence? They're both kind of medieval-ish (hence the confusion, no doubt), so maybe a character in one of those silly stories will throw down that one kind of "gauntlet" and run the other kind of gauntlet.

**The millisecond of ambiguity** is the rationale behind my policy of strictly hyphenating compound modifiers. If I simply wrote *white truffle purveyors*, you would briefly wonder whether the purveyors were white, and you'd have to backtrack and mentally insert the hyphen that applies the whiteness to the truffles. The principle also explains why I'm less likely than a lot of writers and editors to omit the allegedly needless word *that*. Consider the sentence "He believed his wife lied." You're reading along, minding your own business, and you're told that the guy believed his wife. And then—*zing!*—the sentence makes a U-turn and tells you the exact opposite. He believed *that* his wife lied.

**Jumping the gun** is just what it sounds like. Newfangled usages send a message of informality, and sometimes that isn't the message you intend to send. The classic example of balancing the past, present and future is how to use the verb *to graduate*. Your grandmother *was graduated from high school*, and your children or grandchildren might *graduate high school*, but educated grown-ups at this point in history talk about *graduating from high school*.

**Collateral damage** is something to look for as you decide whether to resist a variant form. If it's fine to say *try and* when you mean *try to*, for instance, then what are the inflected forms? You tried and do something? You tried and did something? There's no good answer, and that's one reason the literally correct *try to* is worth enforcing. I'll cover this later in the Curmudgeon's Stylebook, but a similar thing happens if you accept the *mic* spelling of *mike*, meaning *microphone*. If you're wearing a *mic*, are you *miced*? *Micced*? *Mic'd*? Or are you *miked*, and if so, why not just admit you're wearing a *mike*?

**The living legend** is a case in which a disputed variant form has gained popularity but the original, above-reproach form is still very much alive. *It's right there in front of you*, you may have heard me say about *couldn't care less*, for starters.

**"Crazies win"** is not my term; I'm borrowing it from the learned linguist Arnold Zwicky. But while Zwicky, as you might guess, is opposed to letting the crazies win, I think it's a necessary evil. It's essentially the same idea as Bryan Garner's *skunked term*: Sometimes you just want to avoid the issue.

**No footnotes** is a corollary; it's one of the reasons I let the crazies win. If you're writing in a medium that allows you to explain yourself, you can be bold about the conventions you follow. If not, you'll sometimes want to dial things back a notch and stick with norms you don't necessarily agree with.

**The reservoir of goodwill**, on the other hand, is an argument for boldness—in small doses. When the apologists cheerlead for acceptance of a disputed usage by pointing out that notables from Willa

Cather to Jacqueline Susann did it, they're leaving out a crucial detail: context. It's not hard to find examples of great writers breaking the so-called rules, but they tend to do it while *not* breaking myriad other ones. An aura of competence and credibility emerges, and any distraction to your readers is kept to a minimum.

**Distracting and detracting** is what happens when the aura that emerges is one of sloppiness. Distract the readers enough and you detract from your credibility. I'm not on board with everything in *The Elements of Style*, as I'll elaborate on later, but a six-word Strunkism hints at my philosophy here: *Prefer the standard to the offbeat.*

Now, as it happens, Offbeat is my middle name (William Offbeat Walsh—WOW!), and so I'll don my green eyeshade and offer a minor edit: *Be offbeat only when you mean to be offbeat.*

Intention is everything. There's humor, and then there's unintentional humor. There's action-packed entertainment, and then there's the train wreck. If you're a comely lass displaying what's under your shirt because it's Mardi Gras and you're on Bourbon Street and you'd like some beads, please, or because it's the night shift and you're on the schedule and it's your turn on stage at the Spearmint Rhino, more power to you. But if you're minding your own business walking down the street and you simply don't realize your buttons have popped off, I will helpfully point out the unintended distraction. (Or maybe that's a bad example.)

Know the rules before you break them, as the cliche goes, and that includes the first rule of Write Club: There are no rules. Or maybe there are some, but no two of us can agree on just what they are. So you should know the *issues*, the things that may or may not be rules, and decide your position on them. Sometimes your position will be in the mainstream. Other times it won't be and you'll have to decide whether to take a principled stand or whether it's easier to just avoid the issue.

If you're using "I could care less" and "My head literally exploded" because you're trying to affect a breezy manner, or you're simply dashing off a casual e-mail, or you're a learned linguist trying to show how just-folks you are, or your head literally exploded, go right ahead. (In the latter case, I can totally understand why you could care less.) If you're writing something of some importance and choosing those words because you don't know what words mean, I will helpfully point out that you may be sending a message you'd rather not send.

In the coming chapters, I'll argue for maintaining some tiny distinctions and rejecting some fairly well-established usages in the name of distracting as few readers as possible. I'll even argue *for* some new usages because the traditional ones have become so antique as to be distracting. But there's no pleasing everybody, and so we have to pick our battles in the war on distraction.

### A DICTIONARY DISSENT

*Hardworking, hard-working*

Why not give a job to the hard-working hyphen? *American Heritage* does, if I can take its lack of a *hardworking* entry to mean it's displaying the good sense that *Webster's New World* and *Merriam-Webster* lack in this case.

## The Usual Suspects

*Could care less* and the non-literal *literal* are just two of the evergreens in the picky-about-the-language biz, disputed or evolving usages that separate the eager from the hesitant when it comes to language change. It's tempting to treat all these disputes as one and the same, as I just sort of did (or "one *in* the same," as people who like to be wrong would say), but that's an oversimplification. These disputes run the gamut from outright errors (*your* for *you're*) to errors on which some are giving up (*infer* for *imply*) to errors gaining traction (*hone in* for *home in*, *straight-laced* for *strait-laced*) to useful evolution in progress (*bemused* for "wryly amused") to useful evolution that's well established (*host* as a verb, *gender* for *sex*) to the displacement of antiquated words (*careen* for *career*) to the rejection of unfounded superstitions (*hopefully* as a sentence adverb). And I've probably missed a category or two.

It's unlikely that any two people will display identical linguistic fingerprints—personal stylebooks, you could say—as they tick off their stances on these questions. As we saw with *literally*, even the learned linguists have their aversions.

Some will say these issues are *shibboleths*—questions on which the right answer establishes you as a member of a select group. That's true in a sense, but you won't catch me pronouncing *shibboleth* with such disgust that spittle flies from my mouth. A shibboleth isn't necessarily a bad thing. For instance, although there's no longer any reason for newspaper copy editors to use the spellings *hed* for head-as-in-headline and *lede* for lead-as-in-lead-paragraph, I would be wary of hiring a copy editor who was not aware of those spellings. The shibboleth can be a shortcut, the tip of a knowledge iceberg. The select group it's putting you in could be the group of people who know what the hell they're doing.

Reject *whom* in many of its traditional roles if you like (I do), but if you're a native speaker of English and you tell me you had no idea the word even existed, I'm going to make some inferences about how smart you are. The same is true, to varying degrees, about many of the disputes I discuss in this chapter and this book.

In the Internet age, when you're likely to "meet" far more people than you actually meet, the way you use language will be the only clue most of those people have about your intelligence and your capabilities. So it's a good idea to have a working knowledge of the flash points. What follows is a by-no-means-comprehensive survey.

## ATTORNEY

I've heard it argued that lawyers call themselves *attorneys* because it sounds less unsavory. I'm not sure I buy that, but "I'm an attorney" does have a whiff of pretentiousness that "I'm a lawyer" does not. Given that the words are typically alternated for the sake of variety anyway, I think this is an ideal place for my version of elegant variation. Instead of picking one or the other at random, use *lawyer* to mean a person licensed to practice law and use *attorney* to mean "one who represents." I've heard this distinction phrased as "An attorney is a lawyer with a client," but that's not quite right. It depends on the thought being expressed. If you can substitute *representative* and the sentence makes sense and is not redundant, use *attorney*; otherwise, use *lawyer*. So it would be "Sheppard's attorney, F. Lee Bailey" but "Sheppard was represented by F. Lee Bailey, then a little-known *lawyer*." Also: "Bailey, a lawyer representing Sheppard," because *an attorney representing*—a representative representing—would be redundant. Yes, that's a lot of explanation for what most would consider a bogus distinction. Repeat after me: *tiny acts*.

## A BUREAUCRATIC BUNGLE

### *GAO*

It used to be the General Accounting Office. Now it's the Government Accountability Office.

---

## BEGGING THE QUESTION

*Begging the question is a bad idea because it is incorrect.* That, pretty much, is what begging the question is: You assume your conclusion in your premise. It's true that the technical term for a logical fallacy doesn't come up a whole heck of a lot outside college philosophy departments, and you could point out that my argument for *data* as a singular noun (that *datum* doesn't come up a whole heck of a lot in the real world) would also seem to support the use of *beg the question* to mean *raise the question,* but, well, this is my book.

Oops—that's a different logical fallacy. How's this: *Raising the question* is still alive and well. *Brings up a question* is also readily available. I'm all for useful evolution, but to toss out a rather nifty, if rarely employed, term just to have yet another way of saying something ordinary strikes me as a foolish economy. If I say something and you respond, "That begs the question," I'm left hanging to see whether you're finished accusing me of circular reasoning or whether you're simply pausing before continuing your thought about a question raised. Does this happen to me a lot? Well, no. I don't get accused of ad hominem arguments much either (except by *total a-holes!*), but that doesn't mean I think we should start using *ad hominem* to refer to the beefcake photos in Abercrombie & Fitch catalogues or something. I'm hanging on to this distinction.

## BEMUSED

The established meaning is basically "bewildered." The new meaning, the one you generally hear nowadays, is just starting to join the old one in dictionaries, and I have to concede its utility. Whereas there are plenty of ways to say bewildered, dazed, confused or distracted, I can't think of a single synonym for *bemused* as in mildly and wryly amused. You're not guffawing, but you are wearing a little grin. Perhaps you're a little confused as well—you're not quite sure why your new album is charting in Japan while it's being ignored at home, but it makes you smile.

Here's where I get into trouble: I like this evolution and consider it useful, but I reject the usage for now. It's just too new. Too many people actually know what the word is supposed to mean. If the dictionaries, which are inherently descriptive, haven't recognized a usage, it's not a good idea to get out in front of them. *If the books don't describe, you must proscribe.*

## CAREER

White-flag alert: I wouldn't make a career out of insisting that an out-of-control car *careers*, rather than *careens*, down a street. Strictly speaking, to careen is to tilt. But the "wildly lurch" meaning is too well established to be considered an error; indeed, I doubt a majority of educated English speakers are even aware of that meaning of *career*, or of the disputed status of *careen*.

## COMPRISE

My country *comprises* 50 states. Or *is composed of* 50 states. Or *consists of* 50 states. Those 50 states *constitute* my country. If all those *com-* and *con-* words are too *con*fusing, just say the country is made up of 50 states, or 50 states make up the country. I hope I've provided enough choices to make it clear that there's no need to add *is comprised of* to the menu. Even if the phrase has been used by notables from Lord Byron to Donald Trump.

## DIAGNOSE

White-flag alert: Strictly speaking, it's the disease that's diagnosed, not the person. But I see no harm in using the word the way everybody else does.

## DIFFERENT THAN

Preposition panic tends to puzzle me (I couldn't care less whether you're a friend *of* the downtrodden or a friend *to* the downtrodden), and this is no exception. Yes, we're generally supposed to say *different from*, but I don't consider *different than* anything to get worked up about.

Furthermore, there are cases where *than* is preferable, even required. *The motivation was different for Ali than for Frazier. You have a different perspective than I do. We'll be enforcing the law differently than before.*

Our job as writers and editors is simple: Change *different than* to *different from*—except when we can't.

## DISINTERESTED

*Uninterested* is readily available, at popular prices, so just use it already and save *disinterested* for phrases such as *a disinterested observer*, in which it means impartial.

## DUE TO

Sticklers, this one included, use *due to* only when the meaning is "attributable to." Otherwise we make it *because of*. So: *The game was postponed because of rain. The postponement was due to rain.* You can take this distinction or leave it, but what you don't want to do is go all hypercorrect and ban *due to* entirely just because some object to it in some instances.

## ENORMITY

The group of people who know that the word means great evil or wickedness continues to shrink, but the enormousness of their potential laughter at something like "the enormity of this honor" is reason enough to hold on to the distinction. The word will get plenty of exercise, often in references where it could refer to both evil and magnitude, such as *the enormity of the 9/11 terrorist attacks*.

## ENTITLED

The word can be used in stating the title of a book or movie or whatever, so please don't treat the *AP Stylebook*-banned usage as an error. *Titled* is a syllable shorter and 17 percent less pretentious, though, so if you'd like to choose it as a tiny act of elegance, please do.

## FAST, SLOW

You can drive fast. No, really—I've done it myself. Enough with the *quickly* nonsense: Not all adverbs end in *-ly*, and *fast* and *slow* can be adverbs as well as adjectives.

## FLAUNT, FLOUT

You're *flouting* the law if you're *flaunting* the fact that your bitchin' Camaro can do 110 mph on the freeway. Some are ready to wave the white flag and say you're flaunting both the law and your horsepower. Speed away from such people.

## GAUNTLET, GANTLET

To review: You throw down and/or pick up the *gauntlet*, which is a glove; you run the *gantlet*, which is a narrow lane formed by two rows of people intent on punishing or otherwise tormenting you. The similar spellings and similarly medieval natures of the two words have caused them to merge over time, but careful writers maintain the distinction. It's nice to leave room to talk about picking up the gauntlet and running the gantlet, as opposed to picking up the gauntlet-as-in-glove and running the gantlet-as-in-lane-of-torment.

## GENDER

The term started as a grammatical one (*le stylo*, the pen, is a masculine noun in French, while *la maison*, the house, is feminine). Misguided sticklers will demand *sex*, but you can tell them to go you-know-what themselves. If you say you'll be discussing sex in the workplace when you mean gender in the workplace, you'll get a much larger crowd, but it will be a rather disappointed one.

## GRADUATE

When I hear "I graduated college," I want to answer "No, you didn't." The expression evolved from *was graduated from* to *graduated from*, and it is evolving again, but—at least for now—you call your education into question if you omit the *from*.

## HEALTHY

White-flag alert: Strictly speaking, you should say *healthful*, not *healthy*, when referring to a lifestyle or a diet or a specific food that might make you healthy. "A healthy appetite is often anything but healthful," I say in *The Elephants of Style*. But I think it's time to give up; *healthful* is knocking on the door of the assisted-living facility. Go ahead and write about healthy food as well as healthy people.

## HOME IN

It's easy to see how *hone* horned in on this expression. To hone is to refine, which is not far from focusing, which is not far from *homing* in. Still, with the actual expression alive and well, I will continue to reach for it rather than embrace the error or toss a coin.

## HOPEFULLY

The editors of the *Associated Press Stylebook* have gotten into the habit of staging publicity stunts at the annual conference of the American Copy Editors Society, but in 2012 they thought they were largely staying the course—they had nothing like the *mic* and *website* and *email* bombshells of previous years. Or so they thought when they mentioned that oh, by the way, they were lifting the caution against using *hopefully* to mean "it is hoped that" as opposed to "in a hopeful manner."

Well, they were right about *hopefully* but *wrong* about the re-action. All hell broke loose. Although the copy editors in attendance were largely sanguine, the larger stickler community was divided. Some people were incensed. The linguists, meanwhile, were outraged anew at the reminder that this was even a matter of debate. Sticklers don't place the same stricture on countless other adverbs that can be used to modify entire sentences:

*Mercifully, I had an excuse to leave early.* (Wait, *you're* not being merciful—why are you talking about being merciful?)

*Curiously, the cat didn't show up for dinner.* (Wait, you're not talking about a curious cat . . . )

Frankly (!), it's an odd issue for AP style to even address. AP style is mainly for news coverage, and news organizations generally don't express hope or any other opinion.

## HOST

The objection to *host* as a verb lingered longer than the similar objection to *contact*, but I've never shared those objections, which seem downright antique by now.

## INFER

This is a no-brainer. And by that I mean that people with no brains think it means the same thing as *imply*. Let me rephrase that: It's a common error, and there should be no debate about whether to retain the distinction.

## INSURE

You buy car *insurance* to *ensure* you don't go broke in the event of a crash and *assure* yourself you're doing the right thing.

## ITS AND IT'S

You don't need this one explained to you. At the risk of sounding like an apologist, though, I have to wonder about the sadistic nature of the language gods when I think about how one minute we're lecturing the not-so-adept about how apostrophes are for *possessives*, damn it, and the next minute we're ridiculing them for putting apostrophes in possessives such as *its* and *yours* and *theirs* and *hers*. I'm not calling for a usage revolution, just for a little compassion.

## LAY AND LIE

In actual writing if not casual conversation, I *lay* my glasses on the nightstand before I *lie* down. The past tense of *lie*, confusingly enough, is *lay*: *I lay in bed for half an hour before I realized it was a workday.* I've heard rumblings about crossing this off the list of things to worry about, but that would be a downright futuristic move. Literate people overwhelmingly observe the distinction.

## LIKE

Yes, I try to use *such as* when I'm making an inclusive comparison. *I was a sucker for brunettes such as Valerie Bertinelli and Phoebe Cates.* Many consider this a bogus distinction, and I understand that position. I am talking about *tiny* acts of elegance, and this is a pretty tiny one. If I had used *like* rather than *such as* in my sentence about brunettes, nobody would think I was referring to Barbara Hershey and Mia Sara but not Valerie or Phoebe. But bear with me. I've pointed out that the moral scold and slot-machine enthusiast Bill Bennett railed against behaviors *like* gambling but not against gambling. I've said that while food snobs *like* me consider Old Ebbitt Grill a D.C. tourist trap, I happen to like the place. I've pointed to a deft Psychedelic Furs lyric that depends on the distinction: *I've been waiting all night for someone like you / But you'll have to do.*

## LOATHING

If you *loathe* (hate) change, you might be *loath* (reluctant) to embrace new usages. *Loath* is a relatively uncommon word, so a lot of people understandably (but not excusably) use *loathe* for both meanings. Don't be one of those people.

## MEANTIME

Please precede this word with *in the*. If you want to use one word instead of three, use *meanwhile*. It's a tiny act of elegance. Also, you won't look like an idiot.

## MORE IMPORTANTLY

The traditional advice is to change this to *more important*. The *New York Times* stylebook, for instance, puts it this way:

> **important(ly).** Avoid this construction: *He is tall. More importantly, he is young.* Make it *more important.* The phrase includes an implied *what is* (*What is more important, he is young*). Thus *important* is an adjective modifying *what.*

I've always been skeptical. As with the *hopefully* mess, parallel examples tend to back up the more common usage. Nobody (that I know of) insists on changing "Interestingly . . ." and "Significantly . . . ," but do these usages not work the same way? Come to think of it, what about "Importantly . . ." without the *more?*

Still, I followed along. Then Wendalyn Nichols, then editor of the *Copy Editor* newsletter (now called *Copyediting*), told me she had given up on enforcing "More important." Hm. Then I came across an interesting Mark Liberman soliloquy on the matter on the Language Log site.

Liberman points to *Merriam-Webster's Concise Dictionary of English Usage*. That book isn't always a useful guide for setting style, as it (like some Language Log entries) is so anti-prescriptivist that "apologist" might be a better description, but there's some nice research there, and it traces the "More important . . ." prescription to a 1968 Theodore Bernstein entry in his Winners & Sinners newsletter for the *New York Times* staff. *Merriam-Webster* says Bernstein changed his mind in 1977 and declared both options valid.

Why, then, does the *Times* stylebook still come down on the anti-*ly* side? Well, for the same reason that I'm about to come down on the other side: because it's in the business of setting style. If I get frustrated at seeing *Rumanian* or *axe* in stories I'm editing for the *Washington Post*, it's not because the spellings are out-and-out wrong; it's because the spellings are not *Post* style. Few would disagree that it would be distracting for readers to see "an axe-wielding Rumanian" on one page and "an ax-wielding Romanian" on the next, and so it makes sense to standardize such things.

On the other hand, I'm with the write-and-let-write folks at Language Log when I get questions like "Is it 'a top lawyer *at* the firm,' 'a top lawyer *with* the firm' or 'a top lawyer *for* the firm'?" (Answer: See your primary-care physician about a refill of that chill-pill prescription.) I suppose it's debatable whether the presence of "More important . . ." side by side with "More importantly . . ." is more like an axe-wielding Rumanian or a top lawyer for the firm (when does a consistency become foolish?), but I think it's a good idea to make a *-ly* decision and stick with it.

As I point out in an uncharacteristically wimpy taking-no-sides passage in *The Elephants of Style*, Bryan Garner has an interesting entry on *more important(ly)* in *Garner's Modern American Usage*. He raises the "Importantly . . ." issue, the parallel-example issue (he cites "notably" and "interestingly"), and the fact that the omission of *-ly* just doesn't work anywhere but at the start of a sentence. He concludes:

> The criticism of *more importantly* and *most importantly* has always been rather muted and obscure, and today it has dwindled to something less than muted and obscure. So writers needn't fear any criticism for using the *-ly* forms; if they encounter any, it's easily dismissed as picayunish pedantry.

I agree. Sorry it took me so long.

## NAUSEOUS

White-flag alert: There was a time, apparently, when *nauseous* meant inducing nausea, not experiencing it. If so, that time has passed. (I'm not sure I ever saw the word used that way except in usage manuals.)

## OVER AND UNDER

The non-spatial use of the words does not offend me, but I play the stickler and use *more than* and *fewer than* with discrete countable items (*more than 3,000 people marched in protest*). I'm more casual with units of measurement (*he was clocked at over 100 mph, over 1,000 gallons of oil gushed into the harbor*). Whatever you do, please, please do not change the idioms *just over* and *just under* to "just more than" and "just less than." If you insist on getting rid of *over* or *under*, go with *slightly more than* or *slightly less than*.

## THE REASON IS BECAUSE, THE REASON WHY

As I was writing this book, a fellow copy editor was becoming a *Jeopardy* champion. He was quoted as saying, "The reason copy editors are good at *Jeopardy* is because we read so many different things." One observer pounced, claiming that "grammatically" the copy editor should have said *that* instead of *because*.

I would agree that "the reason is because" and "the reason why" are mild redundancies, and I do try to edit out redundancies, even mild ones, but *grammatically*? This is *grammar*? No, it isn't.

(To clarify on *the reason why*: I'll change "That is the reason why we have that rule" to "That is the reason we have that rule," but not the well-established idiom illustrated by "Cut it out with the whistling or I'll show you the reason why!")

## SINCE

Since you asked, I'll tell you I have no problem with the "because" meaning of *since*.

## STEP FOOT

You *set* foot in a place, or you *step* into a place. The redundant mongrel *step foot* has a longer history than we sticklers would like to admit, having been used by notables from Pearl S. Buck to Alan Greenspan, but it remains a sloppy usage.

## STRAIT-LACED

That's the spelling, not *straight-laced*. The latter is increasingly common, but a lot of people also misspell *supersede* and *stratagem* and *minuscule* and *sherbet*, too. I prefer correct spelling. Maybe it's just me.

## STANCH, STAUNCH

I'm a staunch defender of maintaining the *stanch* spelling of the verb, as in *The paramedic was able to stanch the bleeding*.

## THEY

Once upon a time, this would have been technically correct:

> Each of the 15,000 people in the predominantly female crowd had his own reasons for coming to Lilith Fair.

We've come a long way, baby, and although *personkind* and *womyn* still strike many of us as excessive, there is a strong consensus that defaulting to the masculine pronoun is somewhere south of seemly. So, what to do about it? You could invent a gender-neutral singular pronoun, using *s/he* or *(s)he* or something entirely new. Good luck with that. You could alternate masculine and feminine pronouns, sentence by sentence or paragraph by paragraph or chapter by chapter—or just go with the feminine, since the masculine has had its day. Those approaches, to me, look confused or silly or even patronizing.

The state of the art is to recast sentences to make them plural when possible and to use *he or she, him or her, his or her,* etc., when pluralization isn't possible.

It's not a great state of the art.

The obvious solution is what is known as the singular *they*. When a singular pronoun is required but that pronoun refers to a person of unknown gender or to a mixed-gender group, the gender-neutral plural stands in for the singular. Many, probably most, of us do this naturally in speech. We do it in writing, too, even if our stickler instincts lead us to backtrack and "correct" it.

Here's the part where I cop out in a big way: I support the singular *they*. I'm rooting for the singular *they* to become standard. But it just hasn't become standard yet, and so I just can't use it. When I'm not writing with footnotes that allow me to make it clear I know what I'm doing, I'm a coward. The crazies win.

## TRY AND

Sorry, but I have to enforce this peeve. You try *to* do something. To try *and* do something is to (a) try to do it, and (b) do it, which is not the intended meaning of the phrase. Yes, there are examples of *and* working in similar idiomatic fashion. When you say your soup is *nice and hot*, you don't mean it's (a) nice and (b) hot. When you say you'll get moving when you're good and ready, you don't mean (a) good and (b) ready. But, as with *I couldn't care less*, the literally valid phrase is in circulation. It's right there in front of you. So commit a tiny act of elegance and reach for that phrase rather than the idiomatically defensible but literally nonsensical alternative.

## WHICH

If there's one usage point that crystallizes the sticklers' philosophy, the linguists' philosophy and the points in between, it's the idea that *which* should not be substituted for *that* in introducing a restrictive clause. It is a debate ~~which~~ that will live in infamy.

Most stylebooks and usage manuals present the distinction without comment. *The steak that I ate* is a restrictive usage. The clause defines the steak I'm talking about; it's essential. I'm talking about the steak that I ate, as opposed to all those steaks I didn't eat. In *the steak, which I ate,* on the other hand, my consumption of the thing is incidental. Presumably I introduced the piece of meat in question earlier. A *steak, which I ate* introduces a steak but relegates its mastication and digestion to incidental information; the meat in question could have been introduced without that detail.

The helpful-hint shortcut is the presence of commas. If you want commas, you want *which*. (Dashes or parentheses could play the role of commas: You could write of *the steak—which I ate—*or *the steak (which I ate).*

"Aha!" say the spoilsports. There is perhaps none of our sport they enjoy spoiling more than this, and so you'll find more than a few paragraphs on the subject. Essentially, they say this: If restrictive clauses are never set off and non-restrictive clauses are always set off, and notables from John Steinbeck to Simon Cowell have used the un-comma'd *which*, and this distinction was invented by usage pundits anyway, what in the world is the problem?

To which I answer: *Homina homina* . . .

In *Lapsing Into a Comma*, I stated flat out that those who view this point as a bugaboo are wrong. Today, well, I'm vacillating between wrong-with-an-asterisk and right-with-an-asterisk.*

(*Some descriptivists would also accept *asterick*.)

Bryan Garner takes on the linguists in a little more detail, offering published examples of *which* where *that* would have been right and *that* where comma-*which* would have been right and *which* where comma-*which* would have been right. He also points out that H.W. and F.G. Fowler are incorrectly given credit for inventing the whole thing—that they refined a distinction proposed by others.

Bill Bryson, in *Bryson's Dictionary of Troublesome Words*, offers an example of comma-*which* that should have been *which*—but it has the hallmarks of misguided-stickler copy editing rather than sloppy writing:

> Although there is ample precedent for using *which* in restrictive clauses, the practice is on the whole better avoided. At any rate, on some occasions the choice of *which* is clearly wrong, as here: "On a modest estimate, public authorities own 100,000 houses, which remain unoccupied for at least a year" (*Sunday Times*).

It's easy enough to invent an example in which the reader might wonder whether a sentence should be read as punctuated, with the missing comma indicating a new referent, or whether the *which* points to a missing comma, meaning the clause points to the obvious antecedent:

> And that was my experience in Phoenix. The city which leads the nation in sprawl has another problem, namely auto theft.

But that's not an ambiguity you'll find much in the wild. To the extent that Garner's examples illustrate problems that would trouble those who aren't *which*-hunters, they are comma problems. *Who* and *where* work just fine as *which* equivalents without *that* equivalents—with commas alone to indicate restrictive vs. non-restrictive. It's not uncommon to see comma errors with those words (*Bjorn Borg who won six French Opens*), but those are rote punctuation errors that rarely result in confusion.

Evan Jenkins titled his book *That or Which, and Why*, which might have you believe he'd take the stickler position, but no:

> The Britons' great mentor, H. W. Fowler, favored using "that" in essential clauses and "which" in nonessential, but he has largely been ignored by his countrymen. "Which" occurs routinely in both kinds of clauses in British writing, with no obvious loss of clarity. . . .
>
> Summing up: The that/which rule is arbitrary and overly subtle and ought to be done away with. It is without intrinsic sense, but as long as large numbers of teachers and editors insist on it, we do well to understand it.

Jenkins appears to be suggesting the intentionally offbeat—ignore the rule-that-isn't, but keep the crazies in mind. Do what you like, but also consider just letting the crazies win.

My heart is with the sticklers, my head is with the spoilsports, and my official position is with the aforementioned asterisk/asterick. I think the commas do the restrictive/non-restrictive work and I don't consider the restrictive *which* an error by any means, but I enforce the restrictive *that* for a few reasons.

To draw a line that places a comma wherever there's a *which* of this sort is to build a tiny moat to protect against the comma missteps that Garner, Bryson and I illustrate above. There's an added consistency, too, one that I think rises above foolish.

A little ironically, considering that the Fowlers were British, the restrictive *which* is much more common in the United Kingdom than in the United States. In American English, therefore, it has a tendency to come across as British and/or pretentious. If I see it in your writing, I expect to also see *amongst* and *whilst* and plimsolls and lorries.

Finally, something Garner said on Twitter sticks with me.

> *@BryanAGarner: I'm sick of apologists for using "which" as a restrictive relative pronoun: it's editorially retrograde.*

*Editorially retrograde!* What is linguistically acceptable is not necessarily the right choice editorially. Garner is a lawyer, and I read into that tweet the idea of *stare decisis*, of following precedents. Others proposed the distinction, the Fowlers refined it, and stylebooks and writing guides adopted it, so let's just enforce it and move on.

## WHOM

> *@TheSlot: I'm pleased to tell you today that I've signed legislation that will outlaw "whom" forever. We begin bombing in five minutes.*

I wrote that in a cheeky moment on Twitter, combining an homage to a 1980s Ronald Reagan quip with a tweak at a word I've never much liked. I must confess that it could very well be a gap in my education that led me to part ways with so many fellow sticklers; indeed, I was well into my career as a copy editor when I learned how to use *whom* beyond *for whom the bell tolls* and such. Now that I know what I'm doing, I've come full circle: In my personal stylebook (as opposed to when I'm editing for the *Washington Post*), I retain *whom* after a preposition (*To whom should I send this?*) but I don't bother going through the "Would it be he/she or him/her?" calculus otherwise

(*Who should I send this to?*). And even at the *Post*, I favor the conversational over the formally correct for breezy labels (*Who to call*).

When you insist on preserving *whom* in its full flower, you risk not only sounding like a pretentious prig but also being utterly wrong. I don't have data handy, but I would estimate that between a third and a half of the appearances of *whom* and its cousins are hypercorrections. *Whomever* is particularly susceptible. Sticklers see *Dance with whoever brought you* and think, well, I dance with *her*, not *she*, and they change *whoever* to *whomever*. And they're wrong. That calculus should have been applied to the immediate clause: *She* brought you, not *her* brought you, and so *whoever* is correct.

## A REEL MESS

*"My mama always said life is like a box of chocolates."*

In *Forrest Gump*, Forrest is apparently a stickler for the sequence of tenses. Life *was* like a box of chocolates.

## HAVE YOU MET THE SHIFT KEY?

*The obligatory rant about the Internet ruining everything.*

One message you may not want to send with your writing: Boy, am I lazy and annoying. Or *boy am i lazy and annoying*. The shift key has taken some abuse in its migration from typewriter to computer keyboard, and it's become fashionable to ignore its existence. The standard refrain of "WHY ARE YOU SHOUTING AT ME?" has confined all-caps communication largely to the Internet-newbie community, but all-lowercase prose, often with little or no punctuation, has branched out beyond instant messaging and Twitter and taken over entire blogs and even interoffice memos. You can find blogs *about English usage* that contain not a single capital letter.

With apologies to my dear friends who are among these self-styled e.e. cummingses of the cubicle world, I have to say that I find this habit not only lazy and annoying but also inconsiderate. All-lowercase memos are the sloppy handwriting of the 21st century. They put the writer's comfort above all else. Prose without capitalization is harder to read; vital visual cues are absent. I wonder, frankly, whether some people do it to mask their lack of confidence in their capitalization and punctuation skills. Or maybe they're outsmarting their lazy co-workers by making their communiques more difficult to skim.

And then there's the Internet phenomenon of the cryptic abbreviation. Whether because they're lazy, because they want to make it clear they're part of the in-crowd or both, people on message boards just love to use initialisms rather than waste a precious three seconds typing out what they're talking about. If you develop a new interest, you have to do some work before you can understand half of what's being discussed. *Do they have FPDW at MB? Are you taking your LHT to the WNBR? Will wearing BBBF make it more likely you'll get a PDA or even a BBBJ from your FWB?*

# 9.

# Tiny Acts of Elegance

EDITING LIKE A NINJA

*The best fixes are seamless.*

**I**'m writing this chapter with fellow editors in mind, but in a way anyone who writes is also an editor. Even if we don't take the extra step of checking over what we've written, we self-edit along the way. Either way, the best editing is invisible. Beware of quick search-and-replace applications of style rulings. Always check for unintended consequences. Sometimes, as with a Rubik's cube, it takes multiple moves to get to a place that ends up only slightly different.

## A DICTIONARY DISSENT

*Head scarf, headscarf*

With religious strife and increased diversity putting this accessory in the headlines, headscarf makes sense. American Heritage is alone among the three major dictionaries in specifying the one-word form.

## Ups and Downs

Say you're looking at a reference to *Senate Banking Committee Chairman Tim Johnson* and you realize that the committee isn't actually called the Banking Committee—it's the Committee on Banking, Housing and Urban Affairs. But you don't want to say all that, and so the solution is to lowercase *banking committee*. AP style calls for *chairman* to be capitalized before a name, which leaves you with *Senate banking committee Chairman Tim Johnson*. Uppercase, lowercase, lowercase, uppercase—an extreme example of what I call the downsyUpsy.

Even if you look past the fact that, technically, the lowercasing makes hyphens necessary (*Senate-banking-committee Chairman Tim Johnson*), the downsyUpsy is one ugly bastard. As graduates of my Tiny Acts of Elegance correspondence course (four easy payments of $199.99!) know, this is Rubik's-cube time. If at all possible, re-arrange those words. *Tim Johnson, chairman of the Senate banking committee. The Senate banking committee's chairman, Tim Johnson.* That wasn't so hard, was it?

A writer writing about Ford Motor Co. might decide to forgo yet another instance of the word *Ford* and say *company President Alan Mulally*. In a strict technical sense ignored by AP style, titles used that way, with modifiers, function as job descriptions rather than titles and would therefore be lowercase, which neatly avoids offending my downsyUpsy sensibilities. Although *Ford President Alan Mulally* has no such problem, in that strict technical sense it's just as wrong. The *New York Times*, perhaps the only newspaper that pays attention to such things, would instead write *President Alan Mulally of Ford Motor Company* (the *Times* also eschews *Co.*). The *Washington Post* joins the *Times* in lowercasing (and, where applicable, refraining from abbreviating) titles after the word *former*. Whereas AP style is fine with *former President Gerald R. Ford* and *former Sen. Robert J. Dole*, the *Post* and the *Times* would use *former president* and *former senator*, lowercase.

Virtually everyone agrees that *Coach Joe Paterno* becomes *football coach Joe Paterno* and *Professor Richard Lytle* becomes *philosophy professor Richard Lytle*—the transition from title to job description is more readily apparent in those cases. And I'd write *Officer Bill Gannon* but *police officer Bill Gannon*. A closer call, but probably also lowercase, would be examples such as *movie-star governor Arnold Schwarzenegger* and *first-term congresswoman Renee Ellmers*. Note, for a tiny act of extra credit, the use of *congresswoman* rather than *representative* there. Once *Rep.* loses its abbreviation and capitalization, it becomes a much more generic word. A congressman or congresswoman is a big deal, but a *representative* could be representing a PTA or a garden club or a cellblock.

## Quote, Unquote

Knowing when to close the stylebook is a useful skill. If you follow Associated Press style, you're supposed to refer to the president by title and full name on first reference. But sometimes the first reference is in a quotation.

"Obama is a Muslim socialist who wasn't even born in America," one audience member said.

So, should that be like this?

"(President Barack) Obama is a Muslim socialist who wasn't even born in America," one audience member said.

If you said yes, you may need my 12-step program to break your addiction to stylebooks. The people for whom the first-reference rigmarole is not an absolute necessity will vary depending on the situation and the audience, but it's safe to say the president of the United States is on that list. Most of the past presidents, too. Ali, Sinatra, Hemingway. Bin Laden, Hitler, Castro (unless there's a possibility of confusion with his brother). No need for "(Jesus) Christ" or "Jesus (Christ)." And if there is a need for such clarification, it's better to do so outside the quote and avoid parentheses or brackets:

> "Levin is right about that," she said, referring to Rep. Sander M. Levin, a Michigan Democrat who has served in the House since 1983.

Note, by the way, that the use of parentheses rather than brackets for material inserted into a quotation is an AP concession to ancient limitations on the characters that can be transmitted by wire. Chances are you don't face such limitations, and so switching to brackets is a good exception to make. Otherwise there is a risk of confusion when you reproduce parenthetical asides when quoting written matter.

There are other openings for tiny acts of elegance in what I call the care and feeding of quotations.

When you add to quotes (with parentheses or brackets) or subtract from them (with ellipses), you call your integrity into question. You leave open the possibility that you have distorted the speaker's words. "I really . . . like cannibalism" is a technically correct, if dishonest, version of "I really do not like cannibalism." Inserts range from innocuous to mind-boggling. "That was one [of] the hardest things I ever had to do" clearly helps speaker and reader alike, but what in the world is going on with something like "I really like [cannibalism]"?

Did the person say "eating other people," or did he say "baseball"? My solution, to use a partial quotation, doesn't really solve the integrity problem (and indeed you could have made up an entire quotation), but it at least looks less unseemly. Or more seemly, I guess. You "do," of course, have to "worry" about the "Zagat" problem!

Whatever you do, don't add "insult . . . [to] injury." I see this sort of punctuation way too often:

> The study said the redevelopment plan "lacks imagination . . . [and] will cost more than the city is projecting."

Ellipses suck. Inserts in quotes suck. So hey, kids, let's go out of our way to do both!

If you're introducing a break in the quote anyway, why in the world would you shoehorn a word in with parentheses or brackets right at that breaking point? You'd have to really, really hate partial quotes not to do it this way:

> The study said the redevelopment plan "lacks imagination" and "will cost more than the city is projecting."

## A REEL MESS

*"Frankly, Scarlett, I don't give a damn."*

This error is less common than it used to be. What Clark Gable says in *Gone With the Wind*, of course, is "Frankly, my dear, I don't give a damn."

## This Is the City

Stylebooks tend to list cities that are so well known they require no state or country—"dateline cities," they're sometimes called. The implication is that cities not on that list require a state or country. Vienna and Panama City are on the Associated Press's list, which is fine in most cases but could present problems for readers near Vienna, Va., or Panama City, Fla. Washington is on the list, but I imagine the Seattle and Tacoma papers would add the D.C. part more often than most.

On the other hand, if you're writing for Ohioans, you may not be so concerned about the existence of Columbus, Ga., and your Columbus can just be Columbus, the list be damned. Portland, the one that everyone knows is in Oregon, is left out, presumably because Portland, Maine, is a city of some stature, but it would be downright silly, even in a Maine newspaper, to write about a trip to the Pacific Northwest including a drive "from Portland, Ore., to Seattle." Common sense should also tell you that a story or package of stories need not specify where a location is more than once. Say Kansas City, Mo., and be done with it—if that's in the dateline, the caption can simply refer to Kansas City. Publications tend to exempt nearby localities, sometimes even statewide, from the identification requirement, but this guideline, too, should be applied with caution. A Phoenix newspaper might leave off "Ariz." in references to Bisbee or Winslow, but it might be wise to specify where Cibecue, population 1,331, is. At the *Washington Post* we don't use "Va." and "Md." for places in the circulation area, but I've never heard of Beallsville, Md., and Watson, Va., both less than an hour's drive from home, and I'd go ahead and clue readers in.

### A DICTIONARY DISSENT

*Largess, largesse*

Call me a cheese-eating Francophile, but I'm with common usage and *Merriam-Webster* on this one. I like the *e* that *Webster's New World* and *American Heritage* prefer to skip.

## The El Marko vs. the Finer Points

If you're a fellow editor, listen up. And remember, we're all editors. (Or perhaps you'd like some ammunition to use against your editors.) Sometimes a stylebook ruling or a factual correction conflicts with the goal of presenting prose that sounds as if maybe, just maybe, it was written by a human rather than a machine. The correct answer in such a case?

a. *Shrug. The stylebook is the stylebook, and we follow the stylebook.*
b. *Hey, I'm a human! Perhaps I can craft something that satisfies both requirements!*

You guessed it. The artfully wielded Bic can be mightier than the thick, permanent black marker. Here are some case studies. The details have been changed to protect the guilty.

THE RAW COPY: *She is a teacher at Los Cerritos High School, which offers classes in seven foreign languages.*

THE CATCH: It's a high school all right, but that's not its name. It's something long and unwieldy, like Los Cerritos Advanced Institution of Learning and Culture for All the Live-Long Day.

THE EL MARKO FIX: *She is a teacher at Los Cerritos high school, which offers classes in seven foreign languages.*

I SAY: It's either a name or it isn't. There are some conventions that occupy that middle ground—*Time magazine, Washington state*—but "Los Cerritos high school" is just plain ugly. The fix that requires the fewest keystrokes isn't always the best route. As they say on the infomercials, *There's got to be a better way!*

THE FINE-POINT VERSION: *She is a teacher at Los Cerritos, a high school that offers classes in seven foreign languages.*

EPILOGUE: See? There *was* a better way.


THE RAW COPY: *His next campaign stops are in Sandusky and Cleveland, Ohio.*

THE CATCH: "Silly backwards writer! Everybody knows Cleveland stands alone but Sandusky requires the state!"

THE EL MARKO FIX: *His next campaign stops are in Sandusky, Ohio, and Cleveland.*

I SAY: Give me a break. The way it was written is the only sensible way to write such a thing. If that's a stylebook violation, then the stylebook, as Mr. Bumble would say, is a ass.

THE FINE-POINT VERSION: See "raw copy."

EPILOGUE: You're trying to get me to take early retirement, aren't you?

THE RAW COPY: *The group, which backed the confirmations of Supreme Court Chief Justice John G. Roberts Jr. and Justice Samuel A. Alito Jr., objected to the commentary.*

THE CATCH: He's the chief justice of the United States, not the chief justice of the Supreme Court.

THE EL MARKO FIX: *The group, which backed the confirmations of Chief Justice John G. Roberts Jr. and Supreme Court Justice Samuel A. Alito Jr., objected to the commentary.*

I SAY: Good point, bad "fix." The chief justice of the United States *is* on the Supreme Court, and there's a way to reflect that *and* avoid sounding idiotic.

THE FINE-POINT VERSION: *The group, which backed the Supreme Court confirmations of Chief Justice John G. Roberts Jr. and Justice Samuel A. Alito Jr., objected to the commentary.*

EPILOGUE: Was that so hard? Think, people, think!

# 10.

# My Lovehate With Strunkwhite

ELEMENTS OF DISCONTENT

*Making sense of the big rift over a little book.*

sk a normal person about *The Elements of Style* and, if you don't hear something like "No hablo inglés," you'll probably hear something positive. That's likely to be the case pretty far up the food chain, from people who haven't done any *writing*-writing since high school or college to people who write and edit for a living. When you get to those of us who live to write about writing and editing, however, things start to change. And not only because of all those $19.95 *ka-chings* that could be going to our new books instead of that old one. Geoffrey K. Pullum could scarcely be more venomous on the subject, but even the mild-mannered Patricia T. O'Conner and Mignon Fogarty are critical.

My relationship with Strunk and White, like my relationship with the *Associated Press Stylebook*, has been troubled from the start. (We're not allowed to say "six people" because it would be silly to say "one people"? Um, right. I'm sure a lot of mans, womans and childs will appreciate that advice.) Still, I'm reluctant to join the piling-on. It feels like shouting "Red Lobster sucks!" when your Red Lobster-loving grandmother proposes dinner at Red Lobster. But pile on I must, in my role as self-appointed arbiter of all that's good and not so good in English usage, so here I go. Gently.

I love the *idea* of The Elements of Style. Casual speech is a relatively natural act once you've made it past the toddler stage, but writing doesn't come so easily. People need to be told what to do. And many of those who already know what to do crave further direction. If you've made it this far in this book, you probably fall into that category. Fans of *The Elements of Style* say Strunk and White packed a lot of wisdom into that slim volume. We can argue about how much of the advice is wise and even how densely packed those pages are (there's a surprising amount of pointless droning-on), but it's fair to say numerous points are covered.

And you know what? I'd estimate that most readers of the book could recall maybe half a dozen of those nuggets of advice, tops. Trust me on this one: The typical consumer of language advice doesn't have a tremendous absorption rate. Present company excluded, of course.

And so a book such as *The Elements of Style*, one that's intended as a collection of tips rather than a spelling-out of the style of a particular newspaper, magazine, Web site, publishing house or what-have-you, ends up serving as a pep talk. If writing were tennis, it would be the coach, not the umpire. *Watch the ball. Bend your knees. Follow through.* Just by existing, such a guide gets writers and editors thinking about being better writers and editors. It's a flawed start to an important conversation.

Just don't forget that it *is* a conversation. You're free to talk back to your usage guides. (Funny—people don't seem to have any reservations about telling *me* I'm nuts about hyphenated modifiers, or the hyphen in *e-mail*, or *media* being singular.) Make it an adult relationship. Think of Strunkwhite as a spouse or lover or a friend, not as a parent or boss or god. So when you see "Use the active voice," you're free to react the same way you would if you heard "Always use the spoon with the curlicue handle, honey." (Why is that, dear? I see you using the flat-handled one all the time.)

"Omit needless words"? Sure, pal, but who gets to decide which ones are needless?

## A DICTIONARY DISSENT

### *Place holder, placeholder*

*Webster's New World* makes the term two words by omission, but *Merriam-Webster* and *American Heritage*, quite sensibly, have *placeholder* entries.

## Utterly Debatable Style Choices

A book has to start somewhere, but it's striking that the first two "Elementary Rules of Usage" in *The Elements of Style*—presumably mentioned first for a reason—fall into the category of style and not correctness.

1. Form the possessive singular of nouns by adding 's.

Charles's friend
Burns's poems
the witch's malice

I'm with Strunk on that one, but the vast majority of U.S. newspapers would write *Charles' friend* and *Burns' poems*. That may not have been true in 1918 or even into the 1960s, but I think it's fair to ask that current editions of the book include that asterisk.

2. In a series of three or more terms with a single conjunction, use a comma after each term except the last.

The second principle mentioned is the serial comma, or Oxford comma, which was debatable when the book was published and is debatable today. I have no strong feelings about it—for every example in which it resolves ambiguity I could present a counterexample in which it creates ambiguity—except in series containing an embedded conjunction. My background is in newspaper journalism, and so I generally omit the serial comma, but I include it in something like *the departments of Defense, Education, and Health and Human Services*. Otherwise, a reader unfamiliar with the executive branch of the U.S. government might be left wondering whether the second agency mentioned is the Department of Education or the Department of Education and Health. As with compound-modifier hyphenation, by the way, I treat that as a mechanical rule to be invoked pretty much automatically, not a judgment call in which I must play God and decide what could be ambiguous to you.

## Good Advices

Even the Red Lobster of usage manuals serves up plenty of delicious Cheddar Bay™ biscuits.

There is no defense for such punctuation as
Marjorie's husband, Colonel Nelson paid us a visit yesterday.

Indeed, and yet that's right up there among the most common errors you'll see, in both amateur and professional writing. That's precisely the sort of thing a concise basic usage manual should be pointing out. Likewise:

> A name or a title in direct address is parenthetic.
> If, Sir, you refuse, I cannot predict what will happen.
> Well, Susan, this is a fine mess you are in.

In the era of the "Congratulations Britney!" cake, I only wish that tip were more explicit.

The entry (3. Enclose parenthetic expressions between commas) continues with an excellent discussion of restrictive vs. non-restrictive (a.k.a. essential vs. non-essential) clauses that points out, rather deliciously, that *Jr.* is restrictive and "therefore not in need of a comma." Left unsaid is the fact that a comma before *Jr.* would require a comma after *Jr.*, something you rarely get from people who use the first comma, which puts us back in "Marjorie's husband, Colonel Nelson paid us a visit yesterday" territory.

Unfortunately, the same entry also contains the odd endorsement of 6 *April 1988* as "an excellent way to write a date." Nice try, but that never caught on, and modern editions should drop it.

Elementary Rule No. 7 (not in the first edition of the book, so I guess this is E.B. White speaking) addresses the way-too-common misuse of the colon. It scorns this . . .

> Your dedicated whittler requires: a knife, a piece of wood, and a back porch.

. . . in favor of this:

> Your dedicated whittler requires three props: a knife, a piece of wood, and a back porch.

(Thankfully, the entry does not cover the strange ellipses-and-colon thing I just did there.)

Rule No. 9 (again, not in the first edition) tackles a stickler sticking point. People who know just enough to point to a "subject" and a "verb" and to diagram a simple sentence are forever telling me that *is* is correct in "One of those people who is never ready on time." White correctly calls that a "common blunder" and points out that *are* is correct.

The entry, unfortunately, goes on to spell out the idea, also enshrined in the *AP Stylebook,* that *none* generally takes a singular verb, as in "None of us is perfect." That example could go either way: Not *one* of us *is* perfect, and not *any* of us *are* perfect. But sensible grammarians agree that *none* usually means "not any," not "not one," and thus gets the plural verb more often than not.

No. 10 ("Use the proper case of pronoun") covers, among other things, the hypercorrective use of *whom,* pointing out that *who* is the correct choice in something like "Virgil Soames is the candidate who we think will win."

I could continue to evaluate the book point by point, but you get the picture. There are worthwhile notes, too, on dangling modifiers, parallel construction and the power of placing the important stuff at the end of a sentence. Journalists, so fond of front-loading, of cramming in as much information as possible as soon as possible, would do well to heed that advice.

## A DICTIONARY DISSENT

### *Shtick, schtick*

The major dictionaries list both *shtick* and *schtick* and both *shlock* and *schlock* but prefer the *sh-* version in one case and the *sch-* version in the other: *shtick* and *schlock*. Call me a foolish hobgoblin, but I like the consistency of *schtick* and *schlock*.

# A Relic

The advice on margins and layout is anachronistic in the computer age, and I doubt either Strunk or White would still have qualms about *claim, contact, cope, enthuse, facility, factor, feature, finalize, fix, insightful, interesting, kind of, along these lines, meaningful, nice, to host, to chair, offputting, ongoing, personalize, possess, prestigious, relate to, sort of* or *worthwhile (worth while!)*. And yet those qualms live on. *Update, finalize* and *in short supply* are still derided as business jargon.

Those superannuated superstitions would be fine if *Elements* were a period piece and labeled as such, but no. It keeps getting updated. Alongside the *ongoing, offputting claims along these lines* are examples starring sperm banks and Toni Morrison. And, adding insult to anachronism, the updaters went and *ruined* my favorite passage. In the "Do not affect a breezy manner" warning (I didn't say it was advice that I *followed*), the buffoonish alumni-newsletter writer who used to invite classmates to toss him "a few chirce nuggets" of news now asks for "a few primo items." This makes me sad.

## Read It. Just Don't Live It.

Although I worry a little about Strunkwhite's active-voice fetish and "omit needless words" mantra being used as cudgels, I don't share Pullum's fears about the book's influence. Ideally there would be a warning sticker for the impressionable, but people intelligent enough to care about what's correct should be able to separate the good stuff from the nonsense. As I said, the little book makes for a nice pep talk.

## 11.

# When Jargon Gets Jargony

WE HATE PARROTS!

*Oh, OK? Suspects when there are no suspects, and what the hell is a foam pie?*

t's a good idea, in most cases, to do what the police say. It's not such a good idea to say what they say. Consider this report from my newspaper's Web site, Washingtonpost.com:

U.S. Park Police are searching for two suspects in a Feb. 18 robbery near Dupont Circle.

U.S. Park Police said the female suspect may have used a stolen credit card to make purchases at Dupont Circle stores. Park Police said the two suspects are a black male and white female, both 30 to 40 years old.

Near 6 a.m. in a park near 20th Street and Connecticut Avenue NW, police said the male suspect struck the victim in the head with a fake handgun. The female suspect took the victim's credit card and used it at several Dupont Circle stores. She may have bought food, gift cards and cell phones, a press release said.

The female suspect may have driven a white, 2-door Mitsubishi

Eclipse, police said. The female suspect has brown hair with high-lights, according to the press release, while the male suspect was described as muscular and about six feet tall.

Do you see what's wrong? You may not, given the ubiquity of the error. We learn first that the police are searching for two suspects. So far, so good. But then the article starts describing what the suspects did and what they look like. What suspects would those be? A suspect is a person suspected of committing a crime. In this case, nobody in particular is *suspected*. At some point the police might find a suspect or two, but for now they can only describe the *robbers*. If the police find a man and a woman who who they think were the robbers and arrest the pair, those people will then be suspects (they may or may not be the robbers).

The parroting of police jargon is an occupational hazard for re-porters. Police officers and police spokespeople use *suspect* as a catch-all term for criminals and actual suspects. Part of the reason is that they don't worry about libel or slander—and they tend to think they've caught the right people anyway—but mainly it's just a word they've gotten used to and don't give much thought to. What they're thinking when they say "suspect" is really something more like *subject*. Occasionally they'll mix things up by calling a person an "individual," which at least helps make it clear that conjoined twins weren't involved.

When journalists reach for the term, it's partly because they're just being lazy and parroting the cops but also partly because it has a nice, non-judgmental feel to it. *Criminal* and *killer* and *robber* and *rap-ist* sound harsh and legally fraught—what if we're libeling somebody? The irony is that, while using *suspect* when there are no suspects is just kind of nebulous and goofy, the safe-sounding word actually *be-comes* legally fraught if there is a suspect. The story above attributed most of its information to official sources, but it said flat out that the female suspect took the victim's credit card and used it. If, say, Harriett Sponaugle, 25, of Silver Spring, Md., were in the same story as a suspect, the story would have convicted her of the crime.

Newspapers can be sloppy that way, but TV and radio are treasure troves of parroty goodness. I was watching the 11 o'clock news and saw the TV reporter ask the spokesman, referring to a killing in which the authorities had no idea how many people participated, "Do you think you have all of the suspects in the murder?" What in the world would *all of the suspects* mean? Another time, again in a case with no suspects, the anchorwoman said, "Prince George's County police are looking for the suspect who murdered a District Heights woman."

The *suspect* error can be subtle. Consider this sentence:

He's still afraid, even though the suspects are behind bars.

That's from a story about a case in which the police think two guys went on a shooting rampage, so it's true enough, but the use of the definite article carries some baggage. To say that *the suspects* are behind bars, rather than simply that *suspects* are behind bars, and to imply that this person should feel safer as a result, expresses a belief that the police caught the right people, which an impartial news outlet should not do. Even worse, I observe as I put on my forensic editor's hat, the sentence was pretty clearly written by someone thinking like a cop and using *suspect* to mean *criminal*. He's still afraid, even though *the people who did this* are behind bars. I would have said something like *even though the shooting has stopped and arrests have been made*.

To the cops, weapons are always *produced*, and people are always *transported* to hospitals or to jail. Thankfully it was a law-enforcement spokesman and not a media parrot speaking when I heard on the radio, "The officers made entry to the apartment and made apprehension of the suspect." (I made switching to another station.) The "suspect," by the way, was a guy who had held a bunch of kids hostage in his apartment. He may have been "suspected" of other things, but in a report on the man who was holed up for hours, he is simply "the man." We know he's the one.

The D.C. radio station I occasionally turn to for news is fond of turning adjectives into nouns. The weather forecast tells me how cold it's supposed to get *during the overnight*. The metropolitan area is *the metro* (not to be confused with the subway system, which is the Metro). To the traffic reporters, broken-down and disabled vehicles are *brokendowns* and *disableds*.

Across the country in the other Washington, there was a horrible incident in 2009 in which four police officers minding their own business in a Tacoma coffee bar were gunned down by some guy who walked in. A spokesman for the local sheriff's department said, "It was definitely an ambush target situation. There were two baristas and some other customers in there; none of them were hurt or shot at or aimed at." It was a heinous crime, but it was no ambush. *Ambush* implies an attack by someone who was hiding in wait—the word is related to *bush* and can also refer to the hiding place—but he said it, and that was good enough for a lot of media outlets. Why pick up the dictionary and deprive the audience of such a colorful term?

While I'm fixated on the police beat, others are more likely to point to business journalists for their parroting of jargon. I'm a little more sympathetic. I'm not sure even the business types know what they actually mean when they talk about utilizing paradigm-shifting technologies to task personnel to grow the company.

## A DICTIONARY DISSENT

### *Shoe box, shoebox*

I can live with either *light bulb* (*Webster* and *American Heritage*) or *lightbulb* (*Merriam-Webster*), but there's just no reason not to go with *shoebox*. (Alas, only *American Heritage* is with me there. The online version of *Merriam-Webster* suggests that *cowpox* might be what I'm looking for.)

## Across the Pond

In 2011, Rupert Murdoch was discussing his media-mogul-ness with a parliamentary committee when someone not fond of him pushed a pie plate full of shaving cream into his face. Shaving cream is called shaving foam or just *foam* in the British isles, and here across the pond the TV and radio parrots dutifully reported this "foam pie" attack without bothering to translate for us exactly what a *foam pie* might be. Maybe they had no idea themselves.

Similarly, because the United Nations does business in British English, we hear a lot from the U.N. World Food "Programme" about hunger aid being doled out in the form of "high-energy biscuits" or "high-calorie biscuits." Brits and Americans mean very different things when they say "biscuit," of course, but again nobody bothers to think about this and offer a translation. American newspapers just plod ahead in and let readers think starving children are being given fluffy breakfast baked goods, perhaps with butter or jelly or sausage gravy. Polly want a cracker, fellow journalists? Actually cracker is one definition of *biscuit* in British English—the other, perhaps more common one being cookie. In photographs, at least, the food aid in question does look cookie-like, but I can understand a reluctance to say that starving children are being given "cookies." That has an unfortunate Marie Antoinette ring to it. I'd go with *energy bars*.

When riots happen in Europe, somehow the "water cannon" resist becoming water *cannons* in U.S. coverage. Discussion of "transport" doesn't get its *-ation*. Thankfully *sports* is familiar enough over here that even the parrots make the adjustment from *sport*.

## The Eggcorn

The eggcorn is the province of the Geoffs. Mark Liberman (G. Mark Liberman?) wondered what you might call the phenomenon whereby somebody, having heard *acorn* but not processed it as a single word, pieces together *egg corn*, and Geoff Pullum suggested calling such things *egg corns* (the term quickly became onewordized). And for people with such distaste for lording correctness over the less well educated, the spoilsports sure do make a sport out of the gathering of eggcorns. When I'm feeling churlish, I think of this as the linguistic equivalent of a prude going to art films or lavish Las Vegas showgirl revues to sneak in a little boobiliciousness. But I'm not one to judge, in either case.

One entry in the Eggcorn Database (yes, there's an eggcorn database!) holds special significance: *Old-Timer's Disease* was uttered by a member of my household in the 1970s. See how the eggcorn works? Strictly speaking, to be an eggcorn, the mistaken version of the term has to make a certain amount of sense on its own. That one certainly does. Some others include *site seeing, ex-patriots, a 10-year professor, taken for granite, shoe-in, sound byte, vocal chords, all tolled, veil of tears* and *the upmost*.

Now, here's something that could bring sticklers and spoilsports together. We should have eggcorn trading cards—collect 'em all!

## A BUREAUCRATIC BUNGLE

### *NHTSA*

It's the National Highway *Traffic* Safety Administration, not the National Highway Transportation Safety Administration.

# 12

# You've Been Punc'd

THE STUPIDCOMMA AND OTHER THINGS THAT
MAKE YOU LOOK DUMB

*A zero-tolerance guide to punctuation. Note hyphen.*

Let's get this out of the way first: Just one space between sentences in the post-typewriter world. You already knew that, right? Now for some advanced lessons.

Usage mistakes are often the result of people hearing or reading a phrase, misunderstanding the meaning, and then using it to mean what they incorrectly thought it meant. Punctuation errors can happen in a similar fashion: A reader is used to seeing a certain structure but then applies that template even where it doesn't fit.

The comma, that most flexible of punctuation marks, is particularly prone to such abuse. *Fast Company* magazine used a particularly stupid comma in this sentence about the founder of Chatroulette:

> But the Moscow-born, high-school dropout isn't dwelling on
> the millions of dollars he might've lost.

What kind of dropout is he? Two kinds. He's both a Moscow-born dropout and a high-school dropout. A dropout who is both (a) Moscow-born and (b) high-school. I'm pretty sure that's not what the writer intended. The founder of Chatroulette is a high-school dropout who happens to have been born in Moscow, or *a Moscow-born high-school dropout*. No comma. *Moscow-born* and *high-school* are not, as they say in the grammar textbooks, *of equal weight*. The *high-school* part is more intimately connected with *dropout* than the *Moscow-born* part is. *Moscow-born* describes *high-school dropout*.

For lack of a better term, I shall christen this *the stupidcomma*.

A missing hyphen adds to the stupidcomma fun in a Reuters sentence about "a family-friendly, first-time homeowner community." Let's parse that one: It's a *homeowner community* that's both *family-friendly* and *first-time*. Even if I throw in the hyphen—no charge—we're left with a community that is both (a) family-friendly and (b) first-time-homeowner. Again, the weights are not equal. It's a community for first-time homeowners that happens to be family-friendly, or a *family-friendly first-time-homeowner community*.

When I tweeted the following, one of my Twitter followers took issue with the lack of a comma:

> Why we need capitalization: Because my old navy jacket is neither an old Navy jacket nor an Old Navy jacket.

Obviously you wouldn't want a comma in *Old Navy jacket* or *old Navy jacket*, but what about *old navy jacket*? That one could go either way, depending on the intended emphasis. I'll claim poetic license for that tweet either way, but even in another context it's possible that the color of the jacket is integral to what I'm saying. Perhaps the subject is navy jackets and I'm emphasizing that I'm talking about my old one as opposed to my new one.

### A REEL MESS

*"I vant to be alone."*

Plenty of people use that pronunciation, but Greta Garbo didn't. What she says in *Grand Hotel* is a straightforward "I *want* to be alone."

## The Sporty Stupidcomma and What's Essential

The rote application of a punctuation template can do serious damage to a sports story. Observe:

Despite trailing, 48-30, they came back to win.

Infuriated, she beat her opponent, 6-0.

We didn't win, 4-3; we won, 17-0.

Style for scores can go either way, with comma or without. *They won 14-7. They won, 14-7.* Different publications do it differently. But the examples above cannot be defended on style grounds. *The commas render the scores incidental when in fact they are crucial.* Despite trailing, they came back to win. So what? The point of the sentence is that they won *after trailing by 18 points.* Infuriated, she beat her opponent. So what? The point of the sentence is that her fury spurred her to a shutout (*bagel,* actually, would be the tennis term).

If you're still skeptical, the third example should make things clear. *We didn't win; we won!* No. We didn't win by *this* score; we won by *that* score. No? Maybe a little review is in order: The comma renders a clause *non-restrictive* or *non-essential* or *non-defining*. That's why copy-editing geeks snicker and talk about polygamy if you leave the comma out of *his wife Jane*. Without a comma, *Jane* is restrictive, it's defining, it's *essential* to the meaning, as in *that* wife, as opposed to his other wives.

Another punctuation template that ends up getting misused is the practice of introducing quotations with a comma. *She said, "I'm exhausted."* Too many writers and editors take that to mean that a comma should precede every single open-quote mark. So you see *an, "I'm exhausted" kind of day* and even:

She was a fan of the movie, "Gone With the Wind."

If it's not *a, comma, good day*, then it's not *an, comma, "I'm exhausted" kind of day*. And a comma between *movie* and a movie title, unless you have already referred to a movie or otherwise created the necessary context, means you're referring to the only movie ever made. Remember: The comma means you're providing non-essential information.

## The Comma Splice

I could also have said "using a comma where a semicolon would be correct." This is pretty basic, I think anyone reading this book would be more likely to spot a violation than to commit one. There— did you spot that one? As with virtually all the so-called rules, writers who know what they're doing can violate this one without ill effect. A historical quotation, a proverb and a 1970s TV commercial for the brewski-themed hair product Body on Tap illustrate some exceptions:

I came, I saw, I conquered.

Man proposes, God disposes.

Don't drink it, just shampoo.

If you really wanted to "fix" these sentences, you have a few options. Periods can work well: *I came. I saw. I conquered.* There are also conjunctions: *Man proposes, but God disposes.* And, as I mentioned, you can simply use a semicolon: *Don't drink it; just shampoo.* Or do the same with a dash. I've often wrestled with sentences like the shampoo-commercial one, in which the negative-positive duality seems so natural with a comma, even if it is technically a splice. *It's not a problem, it's a solution.* A semicolon or dash isn't wrong, but I don't think the comma is, either. In this case, I'm a descriptivist. The comma is also appropriate in sentences that begin with an implied "if." *You do it, you fail. You snooze, you lose.* I'm not sure those can even be called comma splices.

## The Yearbook Comma

I'd call this the stupidcomma, but apparently that designation is already taken. Pick up a yearbook from high school or college and you'll probably find this one in more than one photo caption.

Sophomore quarterback, Tom Tunnicliffe, scrambles for a gain.

Tennis player, Paul Chamberlin, returns a serve.

He's just sophomore quarterback Tom Tunnicliffe. He's just tennis player Paul Chamberlin. These are labels being stuck before names; the names are not what you would call in apposition to the descriptions. For that you'd need some articles, at the very least:

A tennis player, Paul Chamberlin, returns a serve.

The sophomore quarterback, Tom Tunnicliffe, scrambles for a gain.

Of course, you'll probably want a little more description if you're using apposition rather than just labels:

The star of the men's tennis team, Paul Chamberlin, returns a serve.

The Wildcats' record-setting sophomore quarterback, Tom Tunnicliffe, scrambles for a gain.

Again, note the distinction between with article and without article when a caption lapses into labeling to save space:

RIGHT: Mikael Pernfors and his wife, Kristina.
WRONG: Mikael Pernfors and wife, Kristina.
RIGHT: Mikael Pernfors and wife Kristina.

## If You Open the Apposition Door, Remember to Close It

Speaking of apposition, this is perhaps the most common error I correct in reporters' copy. Observe:

> When voters in Appalachia, Va. went to the polls on Nov. 2, 2006 they found no functioning machines.

Where, again, is the town I'm reading about? It's in Va., of course, but this sentence says it's in Va.-went-to-the-polls-on-Nov.-2-2006-they-found-no-functioning machines. Which Nov. 2 am I reading about? It's 2006, of course, but this sentence says it's 2006-they-found-no-functioning-machines. You indicate the beginning of a bit of apposition with a comma, but then you have to indicate the end of it as well. It's a Washington, D.C., man, not a Washington, D.C. man.

Speaking of apposition, it's a good idea to skip the comma that some people use before *Jr.* and such (and some companies use before *Inc.* and such). *Jr.* is restrictive, as Strunk and White point out, but moreover—and even if *Inc.* is not restrictive—it would just be a stylistic nightmare to have to open and close all those apposition doors and write things like *Sammy Davis, Jr., bought stock in Amalgamated, Inc., before he died.*

## Semicolons Where Commas Would Do

If you're looking to graft two complete sentences together, you can reach for a semicolon or you can reach for a comma and the word "and." If you have the "and," you don't need the semicolon.

RIGHT: We arrived at the airport early, and we made our flight easily.

RIGHT: We arrived at the airport early; we made our flight easily.

WRONG: We arrived at the airport early; and we made our flight easily.

Sentences that are rather long but are essentially "a, b and c" series also tend to get unnecessary semicolons. My theory is that newspaper copy editors who have been trained not to use serial commas never stuck around for Day 2 of that lesson, in which they would have learned that the preference for avoiding serial commas is not an absolute ban on them, that it's no style violation to stick that comma in before "and" when a sentence gets unwieldy:

WRONG (WELL, AT LEAST UNADVISABLE): The barriers to entry in this sector include higher-than-typical personnel costs, the need for thousands of square feet of space and a sea of well-established firms to compete with.

WRONG: The barriers to entry in this sector include higher-than-typical personnel costs; the need for thousands of square feet of space; and a sea of well-established firms to compete with.

RIGHT: The barriers to entry in this sector include higher-than-typical personnel costs, the need for thousands of square feet of space, and a sea of well-established firms to compete with.

You'd also want to use the serial comma if one of the items in your series contains *and, or* or *but*:

WRONG: She has worked at the departments of Labor, Education and Health and Human Services.

WRONG: She has worked at the departments of Labor; Education; and Health and Human Services.

RIGHT: She has worked at the departments of Labor, Education, and Health and Human Services.

Think of the semicolon as the supervisor you ask for when you've done all you can with a hard-working but ultimately ineffectual comma. Semicolons are quite appropriate in these "a, b and c" sentences when a or b or c already includes a comma:

RIGHT: The bathrooms feature stylish glass tile; deep, luxurious tubs; and heated towel racks.

RIGHT: In the early 1970s, she worked at the departments of Labor; Health, Education and Welfare; and Housing and Urban Development.

Note, however, that two items do not a series make. Our language can't solve all ambiguities, and its punctuation system doesn't provide a good solution when an unwieldy sentence essentially presents a pair rather than a series:

WRONG: She worked at the departments of Health, Education and Welfare; and Housing and Urban Development.

RIGHT BUT AMBIGUOUS: She worked at the departments of Health, Education and Welfare and Housing and Urban Development.

A GOOD KLUDGE: She worked at the Department of Health, Education and Welfare and the Department of Housing and Urban Development.

While I'm on the semicolon, allow me to point out that it should never, ever be the last character before an ending quotation mark—the rules for quote-ending placement in American English call for periods and commas always inside and semicolons and colons always outside. Also, the semicolon is in no sense a sentence-ending punctuation mark; whereas there are instances in which you would capitalize the first word after a colon, you would never capitalize an otherwise lowercase word after a semicolon.

## Hyphens for "To"

It's fine to write *1977-1979* with a hyphen (or an en dash, if you like) in tabular matter or as a single unit: *His 1977-1979 reign was uneventful. She lived in Dallas during that 1977-1979 stretch.* But a *from* requires a *to*. She lived in Dallas *from* 1977 *to* 1979.

## Dollars Dollars

This is probably an absentminded typo more than a conscious decision, but people often use both the symbol and the word—*$50 dollars.* This is a bane of copy editors and proofreaders. This, of course, is wrong 100% percent of the time.

## Single Quotes as "Lesser" Quotes

In American English, single quotation marks are used in place of the usual kind when (1) the quoted matter is within a larger piece of quoted matter and (2) as a typographical device for headlines and the like, subject to a publication's style. There is apparently a misconception that single quotes are also appropriate for such things as nicknames, as in:

*"All politics is local," said House Speaker Thomas P. 'Tip' O'Neill.*

Nope. Tip is "Tip."

### A DICTIONARY DISSENT

#### *Shortlist, short list*

Use two words, hyphenating the transitive verb: *She's on the short list. I short-listed her for the job.* American Heritage agrees with *Webster's New World* (and bizarrely includes the hyphenated version as a variant for the noun, while ignoring the verb altogether), but *Merriam-Webster* backs me up here. Google, on the other hand, indicates that people strongly favor the one-word form.

## Smart Quotes That Outsmart Us

Quotation marks and apostrophes that curl in the right direction are pretty awesome—it's distracting in the post-typewriter age to see the alternative, those ugly, unprofessional vertical hash marks, in print—but smart quotes will go dumb on you if you don't pay attention. Say you're minding your own business, typing along in Microsoft Word and working on a newsletter for your Class of '80 reunion. You type "Class" and "of" and a space, and your next character is an apostrophe. But Microsoft Word has no way of knowing that. You just typed a space, after all, and so it concludes quite logically that what you intend is a single open-quote mark, and that's what it gives you. If you're one of those people who just keep typing, you may well have a future in the lucrative political-campaign-sign or T-shirt industries, but please humor me and type a *second* apostrophe, which Word will conclude quite logically is the close-quote mark. Go back and delete the first one and—voila!—you've got yourself a genuine apostrophe. (If you're wondering why I just misspelled "viola," you're probably also thinking it's the Class of "80," and this book probably isn't for you.)

## Hyphens That Should Be Dashes

This used to be a simple piece of advice: Ordinary people tend to say "dash" when they mean hyphen, but you should know better. The dash is the wide line that sets off a phrase, and the hyphen is the narrow one that connects words. If you need a dash but have only the hyphen at your disposal, as with an olde-tyme typewriter or the basic ASCII character set, you type two hyphens. (Raise your hand if you remember filling in that unprofessional-looking gap by using the "half backspace" key on a manual typewriter.) In many modern word-processing applications, typing two successive hyphens produces an actual dash (sometimes this requires typing a space before and after the hyphens). Whether to leave your dashes "loose" (with spaces) or "tight" is a matter of style. Generally speaking, the more formal the publication, the more likely you'll see dashes without spaces. The loose dashes used by newspapers and other less-formal publications reflect a practical consideration: Typesetting technology doesn't always recognize the dash as a wrapping point, and so without spaces there's the risk that word plus dash plus word will be treated as a single unbreakable unit, which means the line before it could be hopelessly spaced out in justified text or hopelessly short in ragged text. You can police such things manually, but that requires time and manpower that newspapers don't usually have.

The Internet, of course has ruined everything, except in those cases where it's improved things or left things exactly the same. You can create a real dash for, say, your bobby-socks-fetish Web site, but there's no guarantee I'll see a dash. I might see a random series of characters that look like curse words from *Mad* magazine. That phenomenon, I'm told, is known as "mojibake," and it's a problem for smart quotes and apostrophes as well. So you can go back to the two-hyphen approach, but the Web treats a hyphen as a potential wrapping point, even when it's followed by another hyphen, and so you risk seeing your dash turned into a hyphen at the end of one line followed by a hyphen at the start of the next line. For some, the solution to all this is to use a hyphen and spaces. Space hyphen space equals ASCII dash. It's not a development I like (on my own sites, I use two hyphens and take my chances), but it's a trend to keep an eye on.

The hyphen mistaken for a dash mistakenly used as a colon, tight on the left and loose on the right, is a particularly misguided bit of mutant punctuation seen most often in informal communication such as e-mail and handwritten notes and in something more formal—the curriculum vitae.

> GOAL- To optimize my potential using dynamic communications strategies.

Yeah, don't do that. What you want there is a colon.

When I say "dash," by the way, I mean the em dash, not the esoteric little critter that is the en dash. The en is a prissy punctuation mark that I have little use for. I use a hyphen instead in scores and ranges (*The United States beat Switzerland 5-0 in the Feb. 10-12 Davis Cup showdown*), and I am on record as deploring the en's other role, as sort of a time-travel superhyphen. The theory goes that when you see the en dash in *school bus–size SUV* your mind will realize that you need to skip back to the previous space and read the modifier-and-noun combination as *school-bus-size SUV*. Um, OK. How about I just write *school-bus-size SUV* in the first place?

## The Old Half-a-Paren Trick

Parentheses come in pairs. Their usefulness for encasing the letters or numbers used to letter or number a list within running text has migrated into the odd but very common use of a single parenthesis after a letter or number used to letter or number a more formally presented list. A properly formatted list uses full sets of parentheses in the former case and periods in the latter case. Got that? Probably not. Allow me to illustrate.

WRONG:

The ATP rankings at the end of 1977 stood as follows: 1) Connors, 2) Vilas, 3) Borg.

WRONG:

The ATP rankings at the end of 1977 stood as follows:

1) Connors.

2) Vilas.

3) Borg.

RIGHT:

The ATP rankings at the end of 1977 stood as follows: (1) Connors, (2) Vilas, (3) Borg.

RIGHT:

The ATP rankings at the end of 1977 stood as follows:

1. Connors.

2. Vilas.

3. Borg.

# 13

# A Hyphen Manifesto

## THE TURN SIGNAL OF PROSE

*On the quest for reasons not to use a punctuation mark
that should be used more often, and the times even I don't use it.*

One night after work I decided to sit at the bar and try the sushi at a new downtown restaurant that seemed too good to be true. Open 24 hours a day. A great variety of draft beer. A wide-ranging menu *including sushi*. I ordered one of the creatively named specialty rolls, plus some Spanish mackerel and some eel.

When the bartender arrived with my order, she narrated, "The Tiger Fur roll, the mackerel . . . and your water eel."

Water eel? Oh, right. "Fresh water eel." The menu wasn't saying that the eel was fresh (though it *was* fresh, thank goodness); it was referring to fresh *water*. But with the words unlinked (either *freshwater eel* or *fresh-water eel* would work here), a server who's no sushi expert could be forgiven for assuming that the *fresh* was your standard menu hyperbole and *water eel* was the fresh food in question. There, in a nutshell (or rather a seaweed wrapper), is the reason we hyphenate compound modifiers: to make it clear what's describing what.

The *Wichita Eagle*'s excellent Grammar Monkeys blog illustrates the principle with a recurring feature called Why We Need Hyphens. Some samples:

> *Because a heavy-equipment operator is not the same as a heavy equipment operator.*

> *Because hazardous-materials training is not the same as hazardous materials training.*

> *Because 300-odd editors are not the same as 300 odd editors.*

To me, hyphens are to writing what turn signals are to driving: helpful, unobtrusive and far too often considered optional. Many in the odd-editor community disagree. Taking to heart the rationale that hyphens are used to avoid ambiguity, they are forever searching for reasons to declare certain modifiers or sorts of modifiers unambiguous and thus exempt from hyphenation.

### A REEL MESS

*"Mrs. Robinson, are you trying to seduce me?"*

What Dustin Hoffman actually said in The Graduate was "Mrs. Robinson, you're trying to seduce me. Aren't you?"

## Can You Hear the Hyphen?

The proverb of the water eel isn't my only reading-between-the-lines argument for hyphens. Listen to how people read incorrectly hyphenated phrases out loud. One of Geico's ubiquitous TV commercials featured the gecko and a dorky executive going door to door to charm customers, reading to their children, among other things. One line from the fake storybook was about a small car-insurance bill, but the actor—no doubt reading from a hyphen-free script—instead said "small-car insurance bill." Instead of promoting the company's low prices, he was blathering on about its unspecified rates for insuring compact automobiles.

Another ad, a radio spot for a product I can't remember, mentioned "high-energy efficiency" when clearly it meant "high energy efficiency." There, although a hyphen between *energy* and *efficiency* would have helped, it would have been stylistically unadvisable. Still, I think the voice-over artist's confusion is a symptom of a society in which hyphens are optional decorations rather than familiar tools.

## In Search of Exceptions

Talk to most word nerds about the hyphenation of compound modifiers and you'll eventually get to a point where they think it goes too far—a now-you've-gone-too-far point, if you will. A good test for the love of hyphens is *high school*. (When you think about it, everything in life is essentially about high school and tests, right?) If you're like me on this litmus test (I'm acidic), you commit that tiny act of elegance and link up *high* and *school: high-school students*. The *Wall Street Journal*'s stylebook is with me, as is the esteemed Bryan

Garner. Most people and stylebooks are more, uh, basic, allowing the readership's collective subconscious to supply the linkage in *high school students.* And *ice cream cones* and *real estate agents* and *civil rights laws* and *law enforcement officers* and *peanut butter and jelly sandwiches.*

Some stylists try to engineer systems to determine which modifiers do and don't get hyphens. In one such system, *high school* and *real estate* and the like are exempt from hyphenation as *fixed compounds* or *permanent compounds* or *permanent fixed compounds* or *fixed open compounds.* Or *set phrases* or *stock phrases.* Some keep a running list of these compounds, some leave editors to apply that guideline case by case, and some invoke the house dictionary. If a compound is listed in the dictionary as an unhyphenated multiple-word unit, the theory goes, it need not take a hyphen as a modifier.

Open your dictionary and it quickly becomes clear that such an approach still requires a significant "ambiguity" overlay. Otherwise we'd have *abnormal psychology professors, absentee ballot counters* and *armored car drivers,* and I'm not even out of the A's yet. A strict application would also lead to inconsistency: *Oil painting* is in the dictionary, but *watercolor painting* is not, so would you hyphenate *watercolor-painting classes* but not *oil painting classes?*

A more promising test for non-hyphenation (if you like that sort of thing) looks at the parts of speech involved. If the words are the same part of speech (usually a noun with a noun), the hyphen is omitted. Otherwise, it goes in. So the adjectives *abnormal* and *armored* would get hyphens with the nouns *psychology* and *car. Absentee* can be a noun or an adjective, but *absentee ballot* describes the ballot of an absentee (noun) rather than describing the ballot itself as absentee (adjective), and so the no-hyphen policy would appear to come into play. Again, an ambiguity overlay is required.

I spent a few days jotting down the unhyphenated modifiers that I noticed in my reading and editing. I see one case of possible ambiguity, but mostly they offend me with their sloppiness. A tiny, tidy detail is missing:

*Red carpet fashion. Leap year birthday. Pressure cooker fans. Absentee ballot edge. Nose job fib. Culture war politics. Gut check moments. Rock climbing wall. Amateur radio emergency system operators. An early May primary. A lemon curd lover. Crash test data.*

*Webster's New World*, the official dictionary of most newspapers, has entries for *leap year, red carpet, pressure cooker, absentee ballot* and *nose job*. *Red-carpet* is listed as an adjective form, but the other phrases would stand unhyphenated under the permanent-compound test. The parts-of-speech test would agree on *red-carpet fashion* and add *early-May primary* but otherwise validate the sloppy forms.

So you have to ask yourself: What do you do when confronted with something like *Doctor helps car crash victims?* Do you leave it as is because you consider *car crash* a permanent compound? Do you leave it as is, reasoning that no sane person would believe it means the doctor helped a car to crash some victims? Do you hyphenate the compound in that headline, where there's some chance of misreading, but leave it unhyphenated in other instances? Do you hyphenate all instances for consistency in this story but approach other stories case by case? Or do you just recognize that it's a good idea to hyphenate compound modifiers and avoid all that torture?

## A DICTIONARY DISSENT

### *Sunbelt, Sun Belt*

The major dictionaries are unanimous—and nuts—in liking the one-word form. *Sunbelt* looks like a trademark for pastel clothing from the 1970s. I went to college in Tucson and began my career in Phoenix, and I know that the region is the Sun Belt.

## Exceptions to Your Exceptions

Compounds that you might otherwise style as solid or separated have to be rethought once a hyphen intrudes. Even if your style is to write *antinuclear* as one word, you can't very well have protesters wearing *antinuclear-power buttons*. See also *unself-conscious people* and *nonlife-threatening injuries* and *non-interest-bearing* accounts. Here's hoping you can be conscious of your unself bearing some non-interest without having your nonlife threatened. I'd hyphenate *child-abuse activism* where you might write *child abuse activism*, but you can't get away with *anti-child abuse activism*. You might write *tea party groups* where I'd write *tea-party groups*, but *tea party-affiliated groups* has to be *tea-party-affiliated groups*. (Again, there is a school of thought, especially on the more formal side of publishing, that using an en dash instead of a hyphen in compounds such as *anti–child abuse activism* and *tea party–affiliated groups* fills the gap, inviting the tea to the party and protecting the children from abusers who are against them, but I don't buy it.)

In other cases—again, with or without Bill Walsh-style strict hyphenation—solid forms have to be pried apart for clarity's sake. There are small businessmen, but you're more likely to be writing about *small-business men*. Do you really mean that the schoolteacher is elementary or middle or high? That the bookstore is used? I've seen a high-water mark called a "high watermark" more than once. And this: *Reese's peanut buttercup*. Lord help us.

## At the Movies and on the Newsstands

Missing hyphens in the titles of the movies *The 40 Year-Old Virgin* (2005) and *Law Abiding Citizen* (2009) would hardly have raised either of my eyebrows—I'm used to the hyphen getting no respect. But quite a few people took to the Internet to register their disgust, proving that people (a) care about correct hyphenation and (b) have a lot of time on their hands. Those examples illustrate another thing: The idea that ambiguity should guide the use of hyphens is crap. Yes, I do like to leave room. What if someday I *do* need to talk about year-old virgins, and 40 of them? Maybe some twisted bastard will make a science-fiction movie in which it's notable that 40 babies have never had intimate romantic relationships. Or what about a 40-year old virgin? The poor dude got old without the magic of true love or a reasonably priced escort service and has maintained that status quo for four decades now. What's called a *real-estate agent* in the United States is simply an *estate agent* in Britain, and so maybe if I were raiding the free hors d'oeuvres at an open house and I heard the woman showing the house say "to-*mah*-to" where I'd say "to-*may*-to," I might remark, "There's a *real* estate agent!" A Realtor trying to sell a mansion on a huge parcel of land would be a real *estate* agent. Maybe if it's going to be chilly outside but I still want as little weight as possible on my carbon-fiber road bike, I might say, "Where's my light blue jacket?" The jacket's light, not the blue. That's what hyphens do. *Light-blue jacket, real-estate agent, law-abiding citizen, 40-year-old virgin.* But noooo. All those fine distinctions, and a few silly jokes, are lost if writers ignore my Chapter 8 advice and fail to *leave room.*

Still, I have to admit that in the real world there's no ambiguity in *40 year-old virgin* or *40-year old virgin* or *40 year old virgin.* There's certainly no ambiguity in *law abiding citizen.* But we hyphenate such things because, well, because we do. More alarming to me was *Time*'s cover story about "The Only Child Myth." Anyone buying that issue to learn about what the magazine considers the sole misconception about children was sorely disappointed to find an article about something else altogether: a myth about children who have no siblings. What the editors meant, of course, was *the only-child myth.* I fear that someone on the "creative" side thought a hyphen would be all ugly and cluttery.

Please don't tell me you're now stammering, "But, but, but . . . *the -ly rule!*" Sigh. For the record, there is a convention by which adverbs ending in the suffix *-ly* are not linked to the verbs they modify. I follow it, like most editors. What too many editors do not understand is that the presence of those letters does not automatically trigger this "rule." It's *only-child myth* and *family-planning clinic* because *only* is not an adverb meaning "in an on manner" and *family* is not an adverb meaning "in a fami manner." Even when *-ly* is a suffix, it's not necessarily an adverbial one. Note that words such as *friendly, leisurely* and *scholarly* are adjectives—they modify nouns, not verbs. So you might have a leisurely-looking rout by Roger Federer, hyphen and all. I like to play with that reality and turn such adjectives into adverbs, *friendlily* bidding someone good morning or *scholarlily* talking about parts of speech.

*Much* more alarming to me was the irony of the missing hyphen in the subtitle of *Eats, Shoots & Leaves: The Zero Tolerance Ap-*

*proach to Punctuation.* Is that like *A Gazillion Reasons Not to Exaggerate?* Zero tolerance indeed!

To illustrate the realities of hyphen policy, what better than reality TV? Imagine a season of *Celebrity Apprentice* featuring Snooki of *Jersey Shore* fame, John Boehner of Congress fame and George Hamilton of Hollywood fame. Then imagine Donald Trump, as he is wont to do, sending these celebrities to the streets of New York to sell stuff. Let's say that stuff is . . . Trump Super-Duper Cranberry-Apple Elixir. It could happen. Then imagine you're *Washington Post* TV critic Hank Stuever, trying to convey the looks on the faces of pedestrians who happen upon this other-worldly sight.

> *And they emerged from the 14th Street subway station to see three semi-familiar faces, three pumpkin-like heads nodding encouragement from a makeshift vendor booth. These orange juice peddlers would not take "no" for an answer.*

Yes. Orange juice peddlers as opposed to orange-juice peddlers. It could happen. I like to leave room.

COLLEGE FRESHMAN: "We learned about evolution in one of my science classes today."

MOM: "Oh."

COLLEGE FRESHMAN: "Yeah, the professor explained it to us, and then he said the Republicans are morons if they keep supporting presidential candidates who don't believe in it."

MOM: "Wow. That seems a little inappropriate."

COLLEGE FRESHMAN: "I have a *political* science professor."

Now, you might take from that vignette the idea that *political-science professor* should normally be hyphenated, to leave room for the rare case when a science teacher can be described as political. You'd be right up to a point, but this is the time and place for a tiny act of elegance. I'd hyphenate in a quotation or a tight space, but ideally I'd write about *a professor of political science*. There, wasn't that elegant? All this leaving of room might sound silly, but you have no idea how abnormal some psychology professors are.

Ducking the hyphenation issue is sometimes one of those tiny acts, but in many cases it's just common courtesy. One benefit to my strict hyphenation policy is what I call the "Let them see what they've done" effect. I would hope you'd see the folly of the piling-on of modifiers in something like *capital gains tax cut constitutional amendment opponents*, but the properly hyphenated *capital-gains-tax-cut-constitutional-amendment opponents* really drives the point home. If you need that many directional signs, you've got yourself a poorly designed road. To write *opponents of a constitutional amendment that would cut the tax on capital gains,* or at least *opponents of a constitutional amendment to cut the capital-gains tax,* is more than a tiny act of elegance. It's an act of mercy and compassion.

## A REEL MESS

*"We're going to need a bigger boat."*

The line from *Jaws* is "*You're* going to need a bigger boat." (Or "gonna," if you must.)

### A REEL MESS

*"Toto, I've got a feeling we're not in Kansas anymore."*

There was no "got" in the *Wizard of Oz* line. Depending on whether Judy Garland was using a contraction or swallowing a word, she said either "I've a feeling" or "I have a feeling."

## Suspensive Hyphenation

Instead of cluttering up a sentence with repeated common elements, writers often keep their readers in suspense for a few milliseconds and write, say, *10- and 13-year-old daughters* instead of *10-year-old and 13-year-old daughters*. Note the spacing. Beware, however, of the common error of extending that spacing convention to ranges and other cases in which the modifiers are not differentiating discrete elements. Observe:

> The red- and blue-clad members of the Bloods and Crips, respectively.

> The red-and-blue-clad fans of the University of Arizona Wildcats.

The same logic that makes those spacing choices obvious calls for a differentiation here:

> He has 10- and 13-year-old daughters.

163

This should be popular with the 10-to-13-year-old set.

That last one is the tricky one, and almost everybody gets it wrong. Just one set, just one modifier—link it all together. Note that "and" phrases sometimes take spaces and sometimes don't, depending on the meaning, whereas "to" phrases pretty much always represent ranges and therefore get smushed together. I'm not even sure "to" phrases really merit the term suspensive hyphenation.

## Twists and Turns

I'm the kind of person who uses a turn signal before changing lanes even when nobody's watching. I signal a turn even when I'm in a turn-only lane. I drive/bike/walk to the right even when nobody's coming in the other direction. It's obsessive-compulsive, yes, and anal-retentive and—whoops! Somebody *was* there that time. Whew.

Just as you can't predict when a car is going to materialize out of nowhere, you can't necessarily predict how your copy is going to be read—or what it's going to look like once it's been laid out in columns and pages. Maybe people will be reading along on Page 1 and thinking they're being told about a high school and then have to turn to Page 10 to learn that high school was acting as an adjective, not a noun, and they were actually reading about a high school . . . teacher! Or *high-school teacher*, as right-thinking punctuators would say. Or maybe that information is delayed only by the split second it takes the eye to trace from the end of one line to the beginning of another. Or the millisecond it takes the eye to get from *school* to *teacher*. The hyphen is still offering at least a little bit of guidance.

I still laugh about the time I read one word aloud from a restaurant menu, prompting my dining companion to ask, "*Now* what's wrong?" The word: "Cheeses!" (Perhaps I take the Lord's name in vain more often than I realize.) The *cheeses* incident came to mind when I was proofreading a page between editions at the *Post* and came across a line that ended with *cheeses-* followed by a line that began with *teaks*. Cheeses teaks? Oh, right, *cheesesteaks*! You have to watch those line-break hyphenations, especially as publishing systems seem to be devolving rather than evolving. A colleague recalled one that's even funnier: *mans-laughter*. It's not only erroneous breaks that can be funny. As I wrote in *Lapsing Into a Comma*, the word *re-arrested*—arrested again—can be and has been divided as *rear-rested*.

---

### A REEL MESS

*"Win one for the Gipper!"*

This isn't so much a misquote as an adaptation, but note that the actual line from *Knute Rockne, All American* is "Tell them to go out there with all they got and win just one for the Gipper."

---

## What This Isn't About

Much was made in 2007 of the *Shorter Oxford English Dictionary*'s removal of hyphens from a reported 16,000 compound words. Another blow against the dying hyphen! People hate hyphens! Yeah, no.

These were nouns, and maybe a few verbs, that the dictionary had previously hyphenated. The move had nothing to do with compound modifiers, or clarity, or sparing readers an instant of ambiguity. It was about British English, not American English. In the land of the dressing-gown, people were apparently still writing about bumble-bees and chick-peas and cry-babies and fig-leaves and ice-cream, using hyphens not seen stateside in many decades, if ever. And it isn't even necessarily an illustration of the onewordization of the language. *Bumblebee* and *chickpea* and *crybaby* are now solid, but *fig leaf* and *ice cream* and *water bed* went from hyphenated forms to two words. British English, at least as defined by that dictionary, isn't moving toward solid forms; it's moving toward American English. And common sense. (Did I say that?)

Want to argue about fig(-)leaf undergarments and ice(-)cream sundaes? Now we're talking.

## When to Refrain

I'm not completely hyphen-happy. In fact, I edit out a lot of hyphens that others would keep. The gecko and the exec in the Geico commercial go *door to door*, not *door-to-door*. *Energy-efficient appliances, energy-efficiency study*, but just *energy efficiency* as a noun. The absent hyphen occupies an entire wing of my Maison du Peeve, but the unneeded hyphen has a pretty big room of its own, a room full of people *ill-equipped* to eat *peanut butter and jelly sandwiches*. I see these people and I think that if they really hated hyphens, they'd leave them out altogether. But there they are inserting them where they aren't needed. They don't dislike hyphens; they just don't understand hyphens. Or maybe I was absent the day my high-school physics teacher covered the Conservation of Hyphens Law.

An arm-in-arm couple is walking *arm in arm*. No need for hyphens. Matters considered on a case-by-case basis are considered *case by case*. No need for hyphens. An up-to-date owner's manual is *up to date*. A burned-out lightbulb is *burned out*. The thing you do at the check-in counter is *check in*. A hard-pressed spokesman is *hard pressed* to explain what happened. It all seems so simple, and yet I read of a company's earnings *growing by double-digits*.

Sportswriters do some particularly confounding things with hyphens. They describe a quarterback after a 26-of-39 passing performance as having completed *26-of-39 passes*. They write of *a fifth-straight victory*. And yet, on the same pages, season-ticket sales, as in sales of season tickets, are described as *season ticket sales*, which would instead mean sales of all kinds of tickets over the course of a season.

Then there's the "Wait—think about it" erroneous hyphen. *Low-Earth orbit*. So it's talking about orbiting a low Earth as opposed to a high Earth? Of course not. It's an Earth orbit that's low, a.k.a. a *low Earth orbit*. Or *color-TV set*. A set of color TV? No, just a TV set that's in color, or a *color TV set*. (Yes, kids, we once watched black-and-white TVs.) I suppose you could make a *grilled-cheese sandwich* by grilling up some cheese and putting it between two pieces of bread, but most people would prefer a cheese sandwich that's grilled, as in a *grilled cheese sandwich*. The grilling of cheese notwithstanding, none of the above would be likely to cause confusion. But how about *private-education loans*? That means loans for private school, but I came across it in a story about student loans obtained from banks as opposed to those obtained from the government. Whereas *selling door-to-door* is a judgment call and *a fifth-straight victory* is a harmless style misstep, confusing the private nature of the loan with the private nature of an education is an outright error. Ditto for *public-health insurance* vs. *public health insurance*.

Some common constructions might appear to be compound modifiers but are not. In *diet doctor Atkins*, the phrase *diet doctor* does indeed describe Atkins, but it doesn't modify. It's merely a label: Atkins was a diet doctor. In *two years' probation*, the equally valid construction *two years of probation* is made possessive. *Six months pregnant* is a strange none-of-the-above hybrid.

I don't hyphenate references to percentages or to *-illion* dollar amounts—*a 20 percent reduction, a $2 million house.* I don't hyphenate terms borrowed from other languages—*a deja vu moment, the per capita expenditures.* I find the idea of something like *McKinley-administration officials* so odd that I advocate a capitalization that I might otherwise disdain—*McKinley Administration officials.* And, of course, proper nouns do not need hyphens as modifiers: *a White House source, the de Gaulle era, an Academy Award winner.* But: *White House-endorsed legislation, the de Gaulle-led movement, an Academy Award-winning actress.*

I tend to omit hyphens in *job hunting, budget cutting* and the like, but *people watching* means something different from *people-watching.* My hand might be shaking if I have to greet one of my idols, but the customary greeting would be *hand-shaking.* Noun vs. verb is sometimes the determining factor: Politicians do their *ribbon cutting* at *ribbon-cuttings,* and I do a little *book signing* at *book-signings.*

## A BUREAUCRATIC BUNGLE

### *TSA*

It's the Transportation Security Administration, not the Transportation Security Agency or the Transportation Safety Administration or the Transportation Safety Agency. Now take off your shoes and step into the I-can-see-you-naked machine.

## Apples and Oranges, or Cherries and Tomatoes?

Sometimes, alas, a hyphen intended to resolve ambiguity instead creates a different kind of ambiguity. Imagine you're at a restaurant and you see that the lovely veal chop you're thinking of ordering comes with *cherry-tomato compote*. Now, that could mean a compote of cherry tomatoes, or it could mean a compote of cherries *and* tomatoes. I have no good answer (*cherry tomato compote* is equally fraught), except to say that, when in doubt, rewrite. Punctuation was simpler before nouvelle cuisine.

And, of course, there's more to life than excruciatingly correct hyphenation. As much as I love Grammar Monkeys' "Why we need hyphens" lines (because a stinky cheese vendor is not the same as a stinky-cheese vendor!), I couldn't resist offering a counterexample:

> *Why hyphens can go to hell: The time I asked the girl at the furniture store for one nightstand.*

### A REEL MESS

*"I'm mad as hell, and I'm not going to take it anymore!"*

The actual Howard Beale quote from *Network* is slightly different—"I'm as mad as hell, and I'm not going to take this anymore!"—though at least one of Beale's followers says it the way everyone seems to remember it.

# 14.

# The Trademark Manifesto

*No, I will not hand you a Kleenex.*
*A Sea-Doo isn't a Jet Ski. Curad doesn't make Band-Aids.*
*Pepsi isn't Coke. Facts are facts, but there's*
*a Jetway-brand slippery slope.*

t was a brave man who first ate an oyster, Jonathan Swift is said to have said. And it was a stupid idiot who first lower-cased Kleenex, I modestly propose.

Sorry—that was a little jerk-y, wasn't it? I don't like to get worked up about these things, but I get worked up about these things. You can add to your "How did this guy get to be such a freakazoid?" tote board the fact that my family never said "Kleenex." It was "Please hand me a tissue." (Actually, we didn't say "please" all that much either, but you get the picture.) So maybe, by nature and/or nurture, I'm disposed to wince more sharply than most insufferable pedants when you talk about band aids and jet skis on your listserv.

Let's start at the beginning: You know the difference between *man* and *Bob*, right? There are words and there are names. A man named Bob is a man, or a Bob, but he's not a bob. A man named Bill in a room with 17 men named Bob is most certainly not one of 18 bobs. And yet that's what people do with trademarks. They're used to seeing water scooters adorned with the Kawasaki name Jet Ski, and so they refer to all water scooters, including those adorned with the Bombardier name Sea-Doo, as "jet skis."

Now, I'm not the speech police. If the people in your family call all tissues "kleenex," as they no doubt do if they're not in my family, that's fine. You like to go jet-skiing and rollerblading in your spare time? Have at it. I know full well that "Coke" for someone placing a restaurant order effectively means "Coke or whatever cola you have." I'm puzzled by the Southern custom of serving Coke cokes and Pepsi cokes and Fanta cokes and Dr Pepper cokes, but I'm aware of it. It's not the only thing that puzzles me about the South. (Isn't Royal Crown Cola all the rage there anyway?) Maybe "having a Coke" and it being root beer isn't all that different from "going for coffee" and getting chai tea, or "going for a beer" and ordering a sex-on-the-beach. Anyway, if you're writing for publication, you need to think about hewing to the facts. Even if Jesus turned water into wine, the Bible Belt's *Atlanta Journal Constitution* and *Hattiesburg American* and *Fort Worth Star-Telegram* don't try to turn Pepsi into Coke.

I'm not necessarily any more fond of big corporations and their armies of lawyers than you are. I will not insist on silly capitalization or the trademark symbol or a mandatory generic addendum: A Big Mac need not be a *BIG MAC*™ *sandwich*. I have no problem with calling Rollerblades Rollerblades if they're Rollerblades. But I do believe in intellectual-property rights (note hyphen). I don't get to set up a grill and open a shack and start selling Big Macs or big macs or bigmacs. I'm all for sticking it to The Man now and again, but refusing to acknowledge fact isn't a good way to do it. Referring to Puffs as "kleenex" isn't much of a populist uprising. It's more like accidentally calling your second-grade teacher "Mommy." (Eben Weiss, the blogger and author known as Bike Snob NYC, observes in *The Enlightened Cyclist* that referring to in-line skaters as Rollerbladers is like calling bicyclists "Cannondalers.")

There are trademarks that people use generically while usually knowing they're trademarks—Kleenex, Xerox, Scotch tape. There are some that are perhaps less widely known but that educated people should really be aware of—Band-Aid, ChapStick, Popsicle, Crock-Pot, Photoshop. And there are some stunners. Did you know about Jetway? Bubble Wrap? Onesies?

Then there's just plain stupidity. You've probably seen a Power-Point presentation called *a power point*. I've read about a house cluttered with *rubber maids*. (It was the residence of a despicable sex offender, to be sure, but I'm pretty sure the reference was to Rubbermaid-brand storage containers and not latex love dolls.) I've seen "whole-foods" tossed around as though that's just what you call upscale supermarkets, as opposed to being a specific chain of them. I've been instructed to toss "a can of rotel" into a recipe. Yes, *rotel*. (There's a brand of canned tomato products called *Ro-Tel*.)

Of course, it's hard to tell these days whether people are really genericizing words that should be capitalized or whether they're just too lazy to reach for the damn shift key. People probably do know the difference between eating in a Subway and eating in a subway (the latter is much more appetizing). People probably don't really think they're making phone calls on a blackberry (even if Ernie on *Sesame Street* did talk on a banana). Is *turtle wax* for my car or my turtle? And the silly lowercasing isn't limited to trademarks: I keep reading about *daisy dukes* (apparently short shorts have something to do with weedlike flowers and lower-tier royalty).

I'm arguing here that using a trademark as a generic term is pretty much always wrong, but some examples are more wrong than others. You probably know that Styrofoam is a registered trademark, but did you know that the disposable cups and plates and packing material we commonly call "styrofoam" aren't even made of the stuff? Styrofoam that's actually Styrofoam is heavier, sturdier stuff used primarily as insulation. As is too often the case, of course, there's no great term that's actually accurate. "Plastic foam" is what we're told to say, but I'd simply make it *foam cups.* Or use paper ones instead.

Perhaps the most puzzling case of a trademark rapidly adopted as generic by the masses is *Listserv.* Like *styrofoam,* the word doesn't mean what people think it means. A Listserv is not an electronic mailing list; it's a brand of software used to create and administer electronic mailing lists. Referring to an e-mail list as a "listserv" isn't simply like referring to an unspecified soft drink as "coke"; it's like referring to an unspecified soft drink as a "coca-cola bottling plant." And screwing up the spelling is no help: Calling it a "listserve" or "list-serve" or "list serve" or "list serv" just makes it a "cocca-colla bottling plant."

Listserv doesn't even fall into the near-monopoly category—you might have trouble thinking of a maker of large trash bins that isn't Dumpster, but the Internet-mailing-list business has another significant player in Majordomo. "Majordomo listserv" would be what I call a *pepsicoke,* in which competing brands are merged so as not to inconvenience those who don't know what words mean. Sea-Doo jet skis. Atlantis jacuzzis. Knox jello. Toast'em pop tarts. K2 rollerblades. Curad band-aids. You get a two-for-one deal with the idiotic but very common "ziplock baggies," which manages to genericize both sides of the equation. Not all plastic food-storage bags are *Baggies,* for the record (shame on you, *Webster's New World!*), and the use of "ziplock" or even "zip-lock" for *Ziploc* won't get you out of trouble, because it's not even an accurate term. Such products don't necessarily *lock* in any real sense, so what you want is something like *zip-top bags.*

It's important to note, by the way, that the genericization of ubiquitous trademarks is far from inevitable—or even permanent once it occurs. I've mentioned the case of *Frigidaire*. And then there are *Scottowels*. More recently, remember when it appeared that *Hotmail* was going to become a generic term for free Web-based e-mail? And I don't hear *Xerox* used generically as much as I used to.

Looking at the cases of brand names that have become generic, you find some interesting stories. Aspirin and Heroin were registered trademarks of the Bayer people in Germany, but they became generic terms as part of the World War II reparations in the Treaty of Versailles. The TelePrompTer people *stopped making teleprompters!* The Thermos people lost their capital letter in a court fight, as did Otis when it tried to protect the rights to the Escalator brand. The escalator ruling held that Otis used the word generically and provided no alternative generic description, setting the stage for *Big Mac sandwich.* It's why the word *brand* was inserted into the jingle that used to be "I am stuck on Band-Aid, 'cause Band-Aid's stuck on me." The logic of that one is kind of twisted: Would anyone think the generic idea of adhesive bandages was blanketing the airwaves with flashy commercials in an effort to persuade people to buy an adhesive bandage, any adhesive bandage? When I get to thinking about people to whom brand names are invisible, I wonder what they would have thought about the running joke in the movie *Repo Man* in which all products were boldly labeled BEANS or BEER or whatever.

The legal background makes it appear, as awkward as *in-line skating* on a *boarding ramp* might be, that there is a refreshing black-and-white nature to at least one battle in the descriptive-vs.-prescriptive war. As long as the U.S. Patent and Trademark Office says Rollerblade and Jetway are protected, you can throw *rollerblades* and *jetways* into the dumpster. Er, Dumpster. There is Coke and there is Pepsi; they aren't Coke-brand coke and Pepsi-brand coke.

But then we get to Ping-Pong-brand ping-pong. Nothing is ever easy, is it?

Now, if they had put me in charge of trademark enforcement a few centuries ago, I'd have kept brands as brands and kept generic terms as generic terms and I'd be fine with Ping-Pong. But we live in a world in which genericization does happen, and that turns my boarding ramp into a Jetway-brand slippery slope. If cellophane and linoleum and yo-yo and zipper failed the test, I feel compelled to step in and say ping-pong also has. You may well feel that way about jetways and dumpsters and even rollerblades. Fair enough.

Here, too, though, the binary bind comes into play. If you're a linguist surveying the vast landscape of usage, you have the luxury of observing that there are Dumpsters and dumpsters and Jetways and jetways and Rollerblades and rollerblades. But if you're in the trenches editing for publication, one decision precludes another. If I say dumpster is right, by definition I'm saying Dumpster is wrong. Or at least I'm saying there are Dumpster-brand dumpsters, which is ridiculous.

The language does back you into corners sometimes. Taser is a brand name for a stun gun, but if I'm quoting the young man who said "Don't tase me, dude," I don't get to change that to "Don't stun-gun me, dude." So I'll write that the way he said it, and I guess I'll lower-case *tase*. I wouldn't use *tase* myself, but in a pinch—say, a tight-fitting headline on a story about a Taser-brand stun gun being used—I could see using the verb *Tasered*, with an uppercase T. Close call, but it's sort of like *Twittering* vs. *tweeting*. And I'm not going to say you can't Google yourself in the privacy of your own home. I'd capitalize that, too, though I'd reserve the right to perform an emergency cap-ectomy if I had to render a quotation like "I googled myself on Yahoo."

I would argue that *a Band-Aid solution* keeps the caps because, in fact, Band-Aid exists only as a brand name, but the emergency cap-ectomy would come into play in a hypothetical reference to "a Curad band-aid." The speaker is making an error, and I'm simply rendering that error the way it makes the most sense. Likewise, even though Jacuzzi is a proper noun, I'd lowercase it if I had to quote a professor saying "There is evidence that ancient man was building jacuzzis." On the other hand, and now I'm really splitting hairs, I might opt for uppercase in "I first heard of this real-estate agent when she left a Frisbee with her name on it on my doorstep," even if the quotation appears next to a photograph of a clearly generic flying disc, not produced by the fine folks at Wham-O.

The hard cases are everywhere. The D.C. chef Michel Richard invented a dessert he calls a Kit-Kat bar. It's not a Kit-Kat bar, of course, but what on Earth would a lowercase rendition of that even mean? Across Washington at Ted's Bulletin, near my house, you can buy what they call a homemade Pop-Tart. I suppose Ted's version is a tart, but it doesn't "pop" out of a toaster. For both D.C. sweet treats, and in similar cases, I'd advise caps and quotes. *Michel Richard's "Kit-Kat bar." The "Pop-Tarts" at Ted's Bulletin.*

Now that I've made my trademarks-are-sacred pitch, allow me to make my trademarks-aren't-sacred pitch. I've written extensively about the silliness of trying to replicate the orthography of brand names. If I had stayed faithful to the packaging of the products I'm writing about, you would have been reading about *BAND-AIDs* and *twitter* and the exclamatory *Yahoo!* Let me repeat: Proper nouns are capitalized. That means initial caps, unless they are acronyms pronounced letter by letter. The occasional one- or two-letter exception is fine, as in *iPad*, but sentences and headings must begin with capital letters, and proper nouns should have a cap at the beginning, or pretty darn close. I don't care what the Adidas logo says; the brand is not *adidas*. I don't care what the Nike logo says; the brand is not *NIKE*. Yahoo and Guess do not get to interrupt sentences with decorative punctuation marks. Packaging is all about visual interest, and if you looked beyond Adidas and the other brand names that people single out for special treatment, you'd find that a large chunk of them use capitalization in interesting ways. They also use fonts and colors that don't get reproduced in actual writing. (*Kleenex* is cursive!) Resist the temptation. Write like a grown-up.

## A DICTIONARY DISSENT

### *Tranquillity, tranquility*

Maybe I was brainwashed by the site of the Apollo 11 moon landing, but I prefer the sleek, modern look of the one-*l* version to the *Webster's New World*-preferred *I llove llamas* spelling, which strikes me as quaint and British. Common usage, at least as measured by a quick Google search, shows that my version is more than three times as common as the officially approved one. (*Merriam-Webster* also lloves llamas, but *American Heritage* is with me on this one.)

# THERE'S NO CRYING IN TRADEMARKS

*In which I argue against my own point.*

Oddly enough, I have a personal example of a case in which the use of *tissues* instead of *Kleenex* caused ambiguity. In Woody Allen's *Manhattan*, perhaps my favorite movie ever, the Diane Keaton character shows up at the Woody character's apartment crying. She mentions needing a Valium.

ISAAC DAVIS (ALLEN): *"I don't think you should take Valium. It causes cancer."*

MARY WILKE (KEATON): *"No. Half a Valium?"*

ISAAC: *"Yeah, abdominal cancer, I think."*

MARY: *"When did they find that out?"*

ISAAC: *"That's just my theory, but I think it's correct. I got tissues someplace."*

Every time I watch that scene in which Woody looks to help his crying girlfriend, I think for a second that he's saying he has biological material, perhaps in a Petri dish in his fridge, to support his theory.

PART THREE

# In
# Good Fun

## 15.

# Return to the Valley of the Retronym

A GIN MARTINI WITH YOUR COWBOY POTATO?

*We have an answer:*
*The egg comes after the "hen."*

In *Lapsing Into a Comma*, I had some fun with the *retronym*—a word that arises to differentiate the original sense of something from a new iteration (the term was coined by Frank Mankiewicz, the former RFK aide and NPR president, who was gracious enough to provide a blurb for the book). Examples are skiing becoming *snow* skiing, skating becoming *ice* skating, guitars becoming *acoustic* guitars, mail becoming *postal* mail and so on. (The "no, we really mean the winter kind" theme continues with *snow sledding*, a term that appears in Andre Agassi's autobiography. Is *non*-snow sledding really that common?)

On a *Simpsons* episode in which Lisa campaigns against light pollution, TV anchorman Kent Brockman announces: "Look out, Matthew Modine and Charlene Tilton. There are new stars in town. *Sky* stars!" I've collected some new retronyms I've noticed in real life. As the world keeps getting weirder, some of them are almost as bizarre as *sky stars*.

Food and drink tend to be a great source of silly examples of these neologisms. If, like me, you're a pretentious bastard, you've probably had your share of duck eggs, perhaps atop steak tartare or a frisee salad, and quail eggs, whose raw yolks are a traditional accompaniment to a sushi roll of salmon roe or flying-fish roe. But if you're tired of such exotica, may I offer you a *hen egg*? (I haven't come across *pig bacon* yet, but there is turkey bacon, so it's only a matter of time.)

And speaking of the health nuts and their perversion of good old-fashioned American standards, apparently at least one restaurant is so deep in veggie burgers and turkey burgers that it feels the need to specify that you can order a *beef cheeseburger*. Another restaurant offers baked sweet potatoes in addition to the usual baked potatoes, and so, in the grand "We have to call it *something*" tradition of *vitamin D milk* and *homo milk*, we're offered a choice of "Sweet potato or *cowboy potato*." Oh, and you can add *dairy milk* to the list of retronyms for non-chocolate, non-skim milk, thanks to an ad for "almond milk."

Not big on those newfangled golden raisins? Well, rest assured that *black raisins* are still available. (I've always liked the British term *sultanas* for the golden ones—here's another reason that's a good idea.) I think you'd know what I was talking about if I offered you some chocolate-chip ice cream, but maybe not. Mint chocolate chip and chocolate chocolate chip have given rise to the delicious retronym *vanilla chocolate chip*.

## A DICTIONARY DISSENT

*Sweat shirt, sweatshirt*

While *Webster's New World* clings to the 1958 spelling *sweat shirt*, *Merriam-Webster* and *American Heritage* are with me and the rest of the world in making it *sweatshirt*.

# The Netherworld

I'm not big on science fiction about teeming hordes living underground, but if you are, you're probably familiar with *the surface world*. Another seamy-underbelly retronym is the term for women who are not porn stars. (Yes, some women are not porn stars. Yes, there's a term for it. And what's the deal with porn *stars*, anyway? Do we need a term for the ones who aren't actually stars, in which case we'll need a retronym for the ones who are?) Anyway, your time is up. We were looking for *amateur girls*. Amateur girls. The amateur variety, I would assume, are more likely to be women whose breasts are not artificially inflated to the size and consistency of basketballs. Yes, apparently the assumption these days is that breasts are fake. If you're female and yours are not, then you're a *natural girl*. Men looking for a not-so-amateur, and presumably not-so-natural, kind of "girl" might pull out *the Green Card from American Express*. Time was, the American Express Card was green, period. Then came the Gold Card and the Platinum Card and the Black Card and the Plum Card and, I don't know, maybe the Periwinkle Card, and so now

American Express has to make its lowly regular-old-card customers feel special.

I'm still wrestling with the porn-star conundrum. (See what I did there? Without the hyphen, you would have thought for a split second . . . ). Some other retronyms are just begging to be invented:

What do you call a non-non-iron shirt?

What do you call a friend who's a friend in real life and not just on Facebook?

What do you call a tweet that has nothing to do with Twitter? (A *bird tweet*, I guess.)

Advances in technology have always been retronym generators, and that phenomenon continues apace. Now that everybody carries a cellphone and every cellphone has a camera built in, the term *independent camera* comes up when, say, some security a-hole is looking for stuff to confiscate in a situation where taking every person's phone away would be impractical.

## Have an Alcoholic Cocktail

Back to technology in a moment. I feel a rant coming on. Let's belly up to the retronym bar for a drink first. Now, a *martini*, as people tend to know if they really put their mind to it, is a cocktail consisting of gin and dry vermouth. Things started to go off the rails when the *vodka martini* (nothing wrong with that name—that's what it is) became more popular than the real thing and people started to simply call it a martini. Cocktail purists had to start asking for *gin martinis*, language purists got vodka whether they liked it or not, and those of us who are both were left with no choice but to increase our rate of consumption. Combine that unfortunate trend with the unfortunate anti-vermouth trend ("*Very* dry." "Just leave the cap on the vermouth bottle and pass it over the glass." "Just whisper the word *vermouth* while you're pouring the drink.") and suddenly all *martini* means is "glass of vodka."

It got worse. Now that all manner of dessert-y concoctions are called *martinis* merely because they're served in martini classes, the menu-journalism community has had to invent the term *classic martini*. You'll occasionally see twists that invoke James Bond or a specific ye olde year or some other marker of superannuality. Order one of these and you might get gin, vodka, both or a choice.

Then there's the daiquiri. If you're younger than 45, you probably don't know what that really means. A daiquiri is rum, lime juice and sugar. Its simple recipe parallels that of the margarita, which is tequila, lime juice and sugary orange booze, and the sidecar, which is brandy, lemon juice and sugary orange booze. (The distinction between lemon and lime when it comes to margaritas and sidecars has been blurred by the unfortunate ubiquity of "sour mix.")

"Oh," you big-city-cocktail-bar-frequenting youngsters are probably thinking right now, "you mean a *Hemingway* daiquiri!" Uh, right. That seems to be right up there with *classic daiquiri* among efforts to indicate that a daiquiri is, in fact, an actual daiquiri. My early drinking life included frozen banana daiquiris and strawberry daiquiris served in large porcelain souvenir vessels shaped like toilets and bathtubs at a very suburban mini-chain in Phoenix called Bobby McGee's (cue Marge Simpson: "An alligator wearing sunglasses? Now I've seen everything! . . . Street signs? Indoors? Whatever!"). I think the place also served *frozen daiquiris*, which meant frozen lime ones the same way *frozen margarita* still does.

Today, at a lot of places, if you ask for a daiquiri without elaborating, you'll get one that's not only frozen but also strawberry. With whipped cream. Try it at a blackjack table in Las Vegas sometime (extra added bonus lagniappe: It's free!). In a perfect world you'd get the standard margarita question ("Frozen or rocks?") plus a query about your druthers in the pulverized-fruit department, but as it stands you're not even likely to hear "Hemingway or . . . ?"

I think the sidecar and my current cocktail of choice, the Negroni, are still safe to order without elaboration. Ditto for the Old-Fashioned, though I'm rooting for the retronym "Don Draper Old-Fashioned" once the chocolate-pineapple version becomes standard. Oh, and what do most drinks come with? *Wet ice.* You know, not dry ice.

### A REEL MESS

*"Why don't you come up and see me sometime?"*

The Mae West line (from *She Done Him Wrong*) almost always gets garbled. She said, "Why don't you come up sometime and see me?"

## Slash This!

*Forward slash.* Forward. Slash. The evil inherent in this retronym may not be readily apparent, so let me explain. The existence of the backslash has made watching television or listening to the radio with me unbearable, because announcers are constantly reading Web addresses and referring to any slash as a "backslash." A backslash, as the name implies, is a *backward* slash. It has a variety of uses in computing and math, but it does not work in Web addresses. What you see in Web addresses is simply a *slash*. Everyone knows what a slash is, right? There is no need for the retronym *forward slash*, which, while not incorrect, serves only to advance the notion that *slash* can mean either. It cannot. It means slash, and *backslash* means backslash. Perversely, in fact, the demise of the simple word *slash* has made the *backslash* error all the more likely. If *forward slash* didn't exist, reading a URL wouldn't become quite as much of a coin-toss event for muddled minds. *Forward slash* is the equivalent of *nontable tennis*.

In a similar computing development, I've started to hear the mouse action that everyone knows of as a *click* referred to as a *left click*. Yes, there is now right-clicking. There is even sometimes a middle button or wheel that can be clicked. But the standard click, if you'll forgive our society's anti-southpaw bias, is the left one, the one under your right index finger. Right-clicking is a special, different thing. The standard slash is the one a row down from your right pinkie, not the one that seems to be in a different place on every keyboard. Let your fingers do the walking. It's a snap.

Some retronyms are just fine. *Guitar* can mean electric guitar, and so I appreciate the *acoustic* clarification. I think ice skating when I hear *skating*, but I realize not everybody grew up in chilly climes. But many, perhaps most, retronyms are a tad infuriating when you're as sensible and logical as I purport to be. Is every single word *that* ambiguous? If I'm reading a Web address and say "slash," are you really going to tell me you have no idea what I mean? I say "slash" and expect you to hear "slash"—if I meant backslash, I would have *said* "backslash." If I said "milk," would you say, "You mean *goat* milk?" If I said "car," would you say, "You mean *rail* car?" If I said "tennis," would you say, "You mean *table* tennis?"

Use your head! (Yes, *body* head, not one of the other kinds.)

## A REEL MESS

*"I'm ready for my close-up, Mr. DeMille."*

The actual *Sunset Boulevard* line is "All right, Mr. DeMille, I'm ready for my close-up."

# 16.

# The *S* Files

CAN YOU ORDER BRUSSEL SPROUTS IN TIME SQUARE?

*It makes plurals. It makes possessives. It holds down*
*a day job as a regular old letter. S is the hardest-working letter*
*in the alphabet. It teams up with the apostrophe, except when it doesn't,*
*to make fools of us.*

**I**f I had gotten off my butt and compiled *The Best Language Writing of 2011*, I would have included a snippet from the comments on the Web site of the *Frederick News-Post* in Maryland, where my brother Terence is assistant news editor. Someone wrote to complain about a local brewery's use of offensive names for its beers (on one occasion, the gentleman reported, a waitress asked him, within earshot of impressionable children, whether he would like Doggy Style or Raging Bitch).

One commenter commented, "Gee, can't you just ask for a Millers?" A reply, from someone using the screen name "fnpposter," went like this:

I don't like Millers, but sometimes get Buds, Coor, Michelobs, Heinekens, Sam Adam, Foster, Buschs, Pabsts, Killian, Rolling Rocks, Natty Bos, Yuenglings, and Molsons.

I accused Terence, but he denied it. Not that he wouldn't have been proud to claim it. You see, the phantom *s* has long been a household topic in my word-conscious family. Before I became an editor and Terence and Kenneth followed suit, we grew up in the Detroit area, where our classmates' fathers worked for "Ford's" and "Chrysler's" (our dad was at General Motors, which, thankfully, I don't think anyone ever called "General Motor"). Everybody shopped at "Kmart's" and "Kroger's." People went to the movies to see Sally "Fields" and Christopher "Reeves."

As the beer examples illustrate, those *s*'s get dropped where they do exist in addition to being added where they don't. For every "Millers" and "Sally Fields," there's a "Snicker bar" and some "Cliff notes." (There were probably some "Burt Reynold" movies at the end of the week back in Detroit, when the *s*'s were starting to get scarce.) I've never understood how hypercorrection results in getting things wrong *every* time—either goils should eat oysters or girls should eat ersters, no?—but that appears to be what's happening. People refer to a single sporting event as *the finals* and a series of primary elections as *the primary*.

*S* is for slippery. Ask Simon and Garfunkel, who must be immune by now to the erroneous pluralization of "Bridge Over Troubled Water" and "The Sound of Silence." (They brought some of it on themselves, though, by putting the latter song on an album called *Sounds of Silence*.) Ask just about any normal person (yeah, my family doesn't count) about the learning curve of figuring out when an *s* does or doesn't get an apostrophe. *Apostrophes aren't for plurals, you idiot!* Then what's with this list of "do's and don'ts"? Why am I getting all A's for minding my p's and q's? *Apostrophes are for possessives!* Well, isn't *its* possessive? Ask a stickler about *Charles's friend* and you'll quickly find out whether you're dealing with an *Elements of*

*Style* stickler or an *Associated Press Stylebook* stickler. (Yes, we have our schisms and denominations.)

Just looking around this punctuation-challenged world can be painful for a stickler. The powerful woodburning union is sticking to its guns, and so we continue to see mailboxes and such announcing the homes of the Smith's and the Jone's. (If you're Lynne Truss, at least you have gigantic royalty checks to soothe the pain.) And then there's the assault on the ears. Every day on the radio I have to listen to a business reporter informing me that "the Dow Jones industrials *is*" up or down. Is "Jeopardy" ever going to let Johnny Gilbert know that, say, $10,801 is read as "dollars," not "dollar"? On one episode of a silly reality TV show about "extreme couponing" I heard about "products that my family use" and about how "The large box of instant mashed potatoes retail at $4.99 each."

Sometimes singulars become plurals as a harmless flourish: *Revenues* for *revenue, profits* for *profit, moneys* for *money* (but please, not *monies*). Sometimes it's a stylebook no-no but a perfectly valid variant: *towards, backwards*. In other cases it has to be considered a mistake. *Abuses* aren't necessarily abuse. *Damages* are related to various kinds of damage, but they're entirely different things.

---

### A REEL MESS

*"We don't need no stinking badges!"*

That's the way *Blazing Saddles* rendered the line, but the original, from *The Treasure of the Sierra Madre*, went: "Badges? We ain't got no badges! We don't need no badges! I don't have to show you any stinking badges!"

---

## The Twist Ending

Words that end with an *s* or even just an *s* sound often confuse people into thinking they're plural. Cars and shoes seem to be particularly prone to this error. *If I win the lottery, I'll buy two Mercedes and three Lexus, but for now I'll have to be happy with my closet full of Adidas and Converse and Doc Martens.* That last one is tricky—the doctor who invented the shoes was indeed *Martens*, not Martin or Marten. The fact that some words ending in *s* do use their singular forms as plurals—*means, series, species*—doesn't help matters. And then there's *biceps*. Everyone talks about a left bicep and a right bicep, but technically speaking there is no "bicep"—the singular word is *biceps*. (Either *biceps* or *bicepses* is acceptable as the plural.)

*S* isn't the only letter prone to the trick-ending phenomenon. *D* and *t* sounds fool people into imagining an *-ed* ending: *I just text you a minute ago. Does your cat like being pet?* This probably explains why we say *roast beef* and not *roasted beef.* It's a wonder *dinging* and *ringing* and *singing* and *swinging* never lose one of their *ings*.

### LOGO TYPES

The corporate world is replete with possessives that omit the apostrophe for the sake of pretty logos: *Starbucks. Popeyes. Quiznos. Harrods. Tim Hortons. Wegmans. Albertsons. Kings Island* and *Kings Dominion. Little Caesars.* (There's also Caesars Palace, but apparently that was a calculated move, to promote the idea that at that casino, everyone's a Caesar.) While this might strike sticklers as cause for head-shaking, it does have one benefit in some cases. Just try making a possessive out of a name that's already possessive. There's still a problem with plurals, of course, although it'd be easier to open two Tim Hortonses than two McDonald'ses.

## OF DIAPERS AND WIPES

"It takes a whole roll of paper towels to do the work of one Handi Wipes," the jingle used to go. This was in the innocent days, before it had to be one *Handi Wipes brand reusable cloth*. (In my family, where my fastidious ways were fodder for mirth, it was "It takes a whole roll of paper towels for Billy to make some tea.") Companies protect their trademarks by choosing singular or plural and sticking with it—subtracting an *s*, or adding an *s* or an *-ed* or an *-ing*, is the first milepost on the road to genericization. You may say "Depends" when you're teasing your friends about their old age and the incontinence that comes with it, but the manufacturer refers to the adult diapers only as *Depend*.

## JESUS!

For some reason, according to many style manuals, even those of us who type *Reynolds's* are supposed to omit that *s* from *Moses'* and *Xerxes'* and *Jesus'*.

## THE UNITED STATES'S?

I protest that the Dow industrials *are* up or down, but the radio guy's use of *is* could be compared to the way the United States *is* or Goodwill Industries *is*. The Centers for Disease Control and Prevention *is*, and the National Institutes of Health *is*. The key difference, I think, is that calling the Dow Jones Industrial Average the *industrials* turns it into a true plural, meaning the companies that make up that average, whereas *United States* and *Goodwill Industries* and the others use plural nouns within larger singular nouns. But even if, like me, you ignore AP style and say *Charles's friend* and *Burns's poems*, you should still treat *States* and *Industries* as plural when forming the possessive. *The United States' love for Burt Reynolds's movies is well documented.* Why? Just because. And you wouldn't really want to type *the United States's*, now, would you?

### A REEL MESS

*"Greed is good."*

A set of ellipses is enough to fix this, but note that the line from *Wall Street* is "Greed, for lack of a better word, is good."

## WHEN JUST ADDING AN *s* ISN'T ENOUGH

Two boys named Billy are Billys, even if they're hillbillies. Rocky and Smoky mountains are Rockies and Smokies, but those are exceptions. When there was a West Germany and an East Germany, they were two Germanys, not Germanies. So BlackBerry devices are BlackBerrys, not BlackBerries, and Treasury bonds are Treasurys, though you might get fewer funny looks with *Treasuries*. And although the *Germanys* principle holds that you don't subtract letters from a proper noun in forming a plural, the usual rules apply when it comes to adding letters when necessary. My people are the *Walshes*, not the Walshs.

## AWKWARD WORD ENDINGS

In yet another exception to the "apostrophes are for possessives" rule, the plural of *do* is often spelled *do's*, as in *do's and don'ts*. The pronunciation miscue provided by the *dos* spelling is not as much a problem as it was when our computers used DOS, but it's an ugly word nonetheless. Sometimes there's just no good answer. If we write about more than one ho (presumably quoting someone less refined than ourselves), is it *hos*? *Ho's*? *Hoes*? Does "No, no, a thousand times no" add up to *nos*? *No's*? *Noes*. (Dictionaries seem to prefer the latter, but good luck with readers understanding that one.)

## THE ADJECTIVAL SINGULAR

Plural nouns sometimes become singular modifiers. You pay a 50-cent surcharge for cheese at that *burger* joint. So, then, are you a *Yankee* fan? *Yankee fan* and *Cub fan* are fairly common, but I prefer *Yankees fan* and *Cubs fan*, if only because the singular doesn't work for all teams. I'm a *Nationals* fan—a *Nats* fan—but nobody is a National fan or a Nat fan.

## INITIALS

Some sports types will argue for *two RBI*, because the plural is stuck in the middle of the phrase *runs batted in*, but I would write *two RBIs*, just as I would write *two POWs*.

## LANDS' END

The clothing retailer is Lands' End, plural possessive, not Land's End or Lands End. Just so you know.

## BACK TO THE WOODBURNERS

If you like *the Smith's* as a plural, you'll love it as a plural possessive. *The Smith's car.* That's right: a car belonging to "the Smith." I guess it could be worse still. You could have a car belonging to the Jone.

## A DICTIONARY DISSENT

### *Town house, townhouse*

I'm not always averse to onewordization—for this term, it's been established for decades. *American Heritage* has caught up, but *Webster's New World* and *Merriam-Webster* are living in the past. (I would extend the solid form to *townhome*, but I have a slight preference for *row house* over *rowhouse*.)

## NO PROBLEM, YOU GUYS

### *Taking offense? It's on the menu.*

I'll get peeved if a restaurant server makes a point of not catching my eye, or makes a big show of not taking notes and then gets the order wrong, or leaves me waiting forever for the check. But I'm afraid I can't join the multitudes who take offense when women are called "You guys," or when "Thank you" is answered with "No problem."

*You guys* is to the more vanilla regions of these United States what *y'all* and *you all* and sometimes *you'uns* are to the South, what *youze* is to New York and New Jersey, what *yuz* is to Appalachia. English uses the same word for second person plural and second person singular, and sometimes *you* just doesn't seem to do the trick. Trust me: "Hi, I'm Brandon, and I'll be taking care of you guys today" is not an attempt to cast aspersions on anyone's femininity.

By the way, when you thank Brandon for delivering your potato skins and fried mozzarella sticks, he should by all means acknowledge your thanks, but there's no law on the books that requires him to use the phrase "You're welcome." That's the tradition, but the increasingly popular "No problem" or "Not a problem" would make at least as much sense. (Speaking of making sense, what sense does "How do you do?" make? I'm fond of Kramer's reply on *Seinfeld*: "I do *great*!")

Now, if Brandon had been delivering caviar and quenelles, you might have had a point in objecting. Fancy restaurants are among the few remaining outposts of old-fashioned gentility, and they demand a certain register that you don't see in establishments that serve potato skins. Otherwise, what's the problem with "No problem"?

And if Brandon asks you whether you'd like your 32-ounce Diet Coke refilled (or Marcel asks you whether you'd like another glass of champagne), "I'm fine" is a perfectly fine reply. You don't have to be named Geoffrey to see that it makes perfect sense as shorthand for "I'm fine without additional liquids, lovely though the beverage was, thank you."

There are plenty of things worth getting offended over in this world; there's no need to invent additional ones.

PART FOUR

# In Conclusion

# 17.

# The Curmudgeon's Stylebook

YOU COULD LOOK IT UP

*Now that I've rescued the endangered hyphen, made the world safe for trademarks and made everyone angry, I return to the grab bag.*

## ABUSE AND ABUSES

Because people love to type the letter s—note how *damage* gets turned into *damages*, or just ask "Sally Fields"—the former is often turned into the latter. The meanings overlap, and so explaining the error gets tricky, but essentially you weaken the term when you make it a plural and steer it out of mass-noun territory. As a mass noun, *abuse* is mistreatment. As a countable noun, *an abuse* is an infraction, a rule violation—possibly a serious one, but probably not a violent one. If you take paper clips home from the office more than once, those are *abuses*. If you beat your child more than once, that is *abuse*, or those are *multiple instances of abuse*. The mass noun can be used to cover both meanings, as in *his flagrant abuse of the paper-clip policy*, but beatings and rapes and harassment are always *abuse*, never *abuses*.

# ACCIDENT

*Accidents will happen.*
—*Elvis Costello*

*Accidents never happen.*
—*Blondie*

This long-roiling dispute in my CD collection reminds me that the word *accident* should be used with caution. It's practically become a synonym for car crash, but not all car crashes are accidental. If there's any doubt, use something like *car crash* instead.

# AFTER ALL

As with *of course*, this is a phrase whose meaning depends on whether it's preceded by a comma. With the comma, it means something like . . . *of course!* It's used to put a fine point on the obvious:

> "You can't let yourself have a margarita? It's Saturday, after all."

Without the comma, it's a statement of reversion to a previously observed reality after a period of uncertainty or a contradictory observation. (How's *that* for a clear definition?) Observe:

> "For a minute there I panicked and thought I had stood you up last night, but then I realized that our date was for Saturday after all."

## AHA

It's already a word. A-H-A. "Aha!" There's no need to cobble together an "A-ha" (unless you mean that band from the '80s) or an "Ah-ha." (I've even seen "Ah-hah.")

## ALL'S

All's I'm saying is . . . what in the world are people saying? (A Google search seems to indicate that "Alls I'm saying," without the apostrophe, is more common, which makes even less sense.)

## ANAL-RETENTIVE

As a matter of fact, it *does* have a hyphen. Thank you for your interest.

## ANNIVERSARY

So many ways to go wrong with this word.

1. Others get more worked up about this than I do, but, yes, *one-year anniversary* is redundant. Make it *first anniversary*.
2. Others, no doubt, couldn't (!) care less about this, but in actual writing you need to come out and say *wedding* anniversary if that's what you mean, the same way you have to say *driver's* license and *telephone* number and e-mail *address*.
3. It makes no sense to refer to the anniversary of an event that

lasted more than a day. There is no anniversary of the Iraq war; what people mean by that is the anniversary of the *start* of the war, or the anniversary of the U.S. invasion of Iraq.

4. *Anniversary*, not *birthday*, is the appropriate word to reach for when the would-be birthday boy or girl is no longer with us. So it was *the 100th anniversary of Ronald Reagan's birth*, not "Ronald Reagan's 100th birthday."

# APOLOGIST

There's the "I'm sorry" apology, and then there's an apology as in an argument in defense of something. If you're an *apologist*, you're offering the latter. You're apologizing if you say, "Oh, I'm sorry about using 'could care less'; I meant 'couldn't care less.'" You're an apologist if you say, "'Couldn't care less' and 'could care less' are interchangeable and have been since before the English language was even invented." Apologizing and being an apologist are essentially opposites.

# AREA

If, like me, you're a fan of *House Hunters* and its ilk on HGTV and other cable channels, you've probably noticed this utter waste of syllables. There are no living rooms or dining rooms anymore; there are *living-room areas* and *dining-room areas*. With other sorts of rooms, you run into *facilities*, as in *locker-room facilities*. If you're looking at an open floor plan (or *open concept*, as they say in Toronto, where the vast majority of house hunting appears to take place for some reason), and the living room and dining room share one space, those phrases are fine. Otherwise, call a room a room.

## ARMED GUNMEN

They're the worst kind.

## ASSASSIN

Some may tell you that *would-be assassin* is redundant, that Arthur Bremer and Lynette "Squeaky" Fromme and Sara Jane Moore and John Hinckley were assassins just as surely as John Wilkes Booth and Leon Czolgosz and Lee Harvey Oswald and Sirhan Sirhan were. Don't listen to them. (When I say *some*, I guess I just mean the one editor from my past who firmly held this belief. But I'm telling you just in case you run into him.) And watch the spelling. Without two *asses*, you've made an ass out of you and me. Which adds up to two asses.

## BASED OUT OF

As jet travel and the Internet have made us more mobile, in both the clouds and "the cloud," language and pretentiousness have moved apace. If you're a creaking relic who actually "goes" to "work," you probably say you're *in* the city you call home. That kind of thinking went out with Bakelite alarm clocks, and by the last decade of the past century, people were merely *based in* their cities. You know, because they weren't wearing electroshock dog collars and were free to move, to roam, even to fly. Now that Palm Pilots have given way to BlackBerrys and iPhones and Android devices and the 20th century has become the 21st, nobody worth his *fleur de sel* is *based in* anywhere anymore. Now we're *based out of*. Citizens of the world are we!

We may pick up our mail in Dubuque, but at any given time, more likely than not, we're in a first-class airport lounge somewhere— even we can't keep track—instructing the Singapore Girl on how to make a proper gimlet.

## BEANIE

A beanie is a skullcap, a hat of small diameter that covers only the top of the head. Some of them have propellers on top. It is not a *watch cap*, *knit cap*, *winter cap*, *stocking cap* or *tuque*.

## BECAUSE

Perhaps you've been taught that the word should not be preceded by a comma? Well, cut it out. Sometimes the comma is needed, and sometimes it isn't. Observe:

"I'm not dating you, because you're ugly."
"I guess that's your loss then. I'm sorry you're so shallow."

"I'm not dating you because you're ugly."
"I would hope not—that would be a silly reason! So, why are you dating me?"

## BIRTHDAY PARTIES

Don't show up empty-handed. That's right: Bring a hyphen. Only a 1-year-old can have *a first-birthday party*, but you may have had your *first birthday party* at 2 or 3 or 47. (The icing-on-the-face thing gets pretty old somewhere between 3 and 47.)

# BLACK FRIDAY

On Black Monday (1987), the Dow Jones Industrial Average fell by 22.6 percent. Black Tuesday, in 1929, was another bad day on Wall Street—a smaller drop but perhaps a more significant one, a crash that came to be known as *the* crash and as the start of the Great Depression. Various lesser calamities have garnered the names Black Wednesday and Black Thursday.

Why, then, you might ask, do Americans refer to the day after Thanksgiving, the start of the Christmas shopping season, the so-called biggest shopping day of the year, presumably a joyous occasion for the nation's retailers, as *Black Friday*?

Or maybe you've heard why—because the Christmas season is so important to retailers, and that shopping day so big, that stores generally don't begin to turn a profit for the year until then. They're in the *red*, as in red ink on a ledger, but after that Friday they're in the *black*.

Well, you heard wrong. Black Friday sounds like a lament because it started as a lament. While I was merely rolling my eyes at the term, the linguists and lexicographers were hard at work researching it. Ben Zimmer at Visual Thesaurus, pointing to findings that Bonnie Taylor-Blake posted on the mailing list of the American Dialect Society, cites a 1951 appearance of the term. The reference is to absenteeism at factories. But it's noted that the term truly gained traction in the early 1960s in Philadelphia. There, police officers bemoaned all the traffic created by all the shopping. Merchants, in fact, hated the term and tried to replace it with "Big Friday." When that didn't work, they started to hammer home the profit angle, either in its current black-for-the-year form or as a broader reference to profits in general.

Especially with its actual meaning but even with its fake one, the term strikes me as an observation made from the outside. A store trumpeting a "Black Friday Sale" strikes me as ridiculous, like an automaker calling the base version of one of its models the Base, or a municipality christening a frontage road with the name Frontage Road. I know I sometimes get too alarmist about such things, but they strike me as another sign that we're losing the ability to distinguish between fact and commentary, between a description and a name.

## BLOC, BLOCK

Because *bloc* means a political alliance, that spelling sometimes strays into *block* territory when the subject is politics, as in the misguidedly spelled "bloc of votes." A block of votes represents a bloc of legislators, at least temporarily, but it keeps its *k*. A *bloc* must consist of people.

## BLOG

The word is a noun meaning Web log and a verb meaning to write on a Web log. It's become so common that some of you are probably thinking, "What's a *Web log*?" I have no fuddy-duddy objections to any of that, but I do have one request: Please stop using *blog* to mean *blog entry* or *blog post*. "Take a look at my latest blog" implies that you had established one or more Web logs in the past and that you recently established a new one. Yes, you could point to each episode or performance of a *show* being a *show*, but *show* is a pretty expansive word. *Blog* is a little word, and it's better that way. A poem isn't made up of poems, a movie isn't made up of movies, a book isn't made up of books, and a blog isn't made up of blogs.

## BLOGGER

The blogger is the one writing blog entries on a blog. People who *comment* on those entries are *commenters*. They are not bloggers. (Well, they may well be bloggers, on some other blog, but that's beside the point.)

## BRAINCHILD

It's an idea that someone metaphorically gives birth to. It doesn't mean a brainy child—a *whiz kid* or *wunderkind*. And it doesn't mean an idiot, as in a person with the brain of a child. Or a particularly stupid utterance, one befitting a child but coming from an adult. (The mistaken usages are rare, but I've witnessed all of them.)

## BRAZIER

A brazier holds hot coals. The thing that holds breasts, even hot ones, is a *brassiere*.

## BUSH, GEORGE

That's exactly what we could have called the 43rd president of the United States. It's his name, after all. The trouble is, that name was already taken. By the 41st president of the United States. You know, his father. Come on, now, it wasn't *that* long ago.

Speaking of presidents, do you remember John Adams? Yeah, *that* John Adams. If I had meant John *Quincy* Adams, I'd have said John Quincy Adams. And when I mean George W. Bush, I say "George W. Bush." See COFFEE SHOP, FLASH MOB and PHONE BOOK.

## BUTTON-DOWN SHIRTS

The term refers to the buttons that hold down the collar, as on the classic Brooks Brothers men's dress oxford; it does not, despite the common usage, mean all shirts with buttons all the way up the front. Call those *button-up shirts* or *button-front shirts* or simply *dress shirts*.

## CACHE AND CACHET

I'm repeating myself here, but this is a scourge that is proving difficult to eradicate. If you're talking about something that carries an air of prestige, like, say, you know, that tattered copy of *Lapsing Into a Comma* that you allow to peek out of the corner of your backpack when you go to editing class, you mean it has *cachet*. That's the one that's pronounced "cash-AY." A *cache* (one syllable, no accent mark, pronounced "CASH") is a hiding place or the contents of that hiding place. A cache of weapons. A cache of drugs. A cache of cash.

# CANNON

One cannon, two *cannons*. If you're using American English and you're less than 150 years old, you form the plural the regular old add-an-*s* way, whether you're talking about boom-boom cannons or water cannons. None of this "The police trained water cannon on the protesters" business. And you, having the good taste to be reading this book, don't need to be told that *canon* is a whole different thing. Alas, not everyone does. Spread the word.

# CAVE

I'm caving on *cave*. I'm on record as objecting to the term as a shortening of *cave in*, but clearly it's become its own thing. People and people-run entities *cave* when they relent or acquiesce; structures and geological formations and the like *cave in* when they, uh, cave in.

# CENTURIES AND DECADES

You might remember a minor kerfuffle as 1999 gave way to 2000, about whether we were in a new century. We were, in the sense that the century we loosely refer to as the 1900s was no more, but we weren't yet in the 21st century. Consider that the first century A.D. began with 1 (there's no year zero) and do the math.

Decades don't do the ordinal thing. Nobody hailed 2000 as the start of the 201st decade; that year simply meant that the 1990s were over and the whatever-you-call-'ems were beginning. Yes, it's weird that we have these two different ways of looking at the passage of years, but don't go confusing them and start insisting that 2000 wasn't part of the 2000s, or that 1960 was in the '50s. That would be silly.

## CHANCE AND OPPORTUNITY

If, like me, you're a fan of tennis on TV, you've probably noticed this utter waste of a syllable or five. There are no game points, break points, set points or match points anymore; there are *game-point opportunities* and *break-point chances* and *set-point opportunities* and *match-point chances*. (That's quite a waste of hyphens, too!) The wordiness is bad enough, but if I put on my Mr. Literal hat I might point out that, really, the point *before* the break point is the break-point opportunity. If you're serving at 15-40, I'm at break point. If it's just 15-30, I'm a point away from a break point. Now, that's what I'd call a break-point *chance*.

## CHIC

This, of course, is the French word meaning stylish and sophisticated, pronounced *sheek*, as in "Le freak, c'est chic!" If you're looking for the slang term for a woman (and, no doubt, raising an "I'm being coyly retro here, so don't be offended" eyebrow), you mean *chick*. Pronounced *chick*, as in "That chick is *chic*!"

## CHILI, CHILLI, CHILE

*Chili* (plural *chilis* or *chilies*) is the standard American English spelling for certain peppers; it's also short for *chili con carne*, a meaty stew made from such peppers. (You can also have meatless chili, which makes perfect sense culinarily if not etymologically.) But you know all that already. You may also know that in British English it's *chilli* and *chillies*. But here's where things get confusing, and tasty: Near the Mexican border, especially in Arizona and New Mexico, the Spanish spelling *chile* is predominant for the pepper and for some different stews. Order a good old American bowl of red at a cowboy bar in Phoenix and it's still *chili*, but a very similar red stew at the Mexican dive across the street is likely to be *chile* both in Spanish (*chile colorado*) and English (*red chile*). Even tastier, in my opinion, is *chile verde*, or *green chile*. In Arizona, that means a stew, usually with pork but sometimes with chicken or beef, in which peppers that are green (but not *green peppers!*) and *tomatillos*, which are like green cherry tomatoes with a paper husk, steer the color away from red, though tomatoes may also be present. Green and red chile are commonly used as burrito fillings rather than served by the bowl in Arizona—oh, and the burritos are often called *burros*. Things are slightly different in New Mexico, where red chile is pretty much the same but *green chile* tends to mean, basically, *green chiles*—ask for it on your burrito and you get a paste of minced peppers-that-are-green. Those takes on red and green chile are called simply *red* and *green* in New Mexico, and they tend to be used as toppings for other things. Order a burrito or an enchilada and you're likely to be asked, "Red or green?" You can order "Christmas" if you want both. If you want Arizona-style green chile, ask for *green chile stew* and expect it in a bowl, not a burrito. The Arizona style can also be found in Colorado.

But I just remembered this is a stylebook, not a cookbook (note to self: Don't write on an empty stomach), and so here's my point: Go ahead and use the *chili* spelling for a general audience, but consider *chile* where appropriate if your circulation is in Arizona or New Mexico, or if you're writing for a food-savvy audience. "Green chili," to those who have had the pleasure of such a burr(it)o, will just look wrong.

# CLAIM

The word is shunned by the Copy Editor American Community, on the theory that readers will inevitably read it with skeptical italics. Think of the "but . . ." you might infer if you read something like "The politician *claims* his actions were innocent." I'm ready to relax a little on this one—a claim is a claim. I am, however, maintaining my insistence that the skeptical italics are an integral part of "so-called."

# COED

When coeducational colleges were still a novelty, female students at such colleges were often referred to as "coeds." As the '60s became the '70s, and the '70s became the '80s, the word did not age well. The term became virtually meaningless as same-sex schools became increasingly rare. It's more than a little sexist to refer to female students as "coeds" when their male classmates are simply "students," and the seemingly obvious original meaning got lost as people referred to women at *non*-coeducational schools as "Wellesley coeds" and "Barnard coeds."

A virtual ban on the word was part of the copy-editing canon when I started my career in the early '80s, but I'm seeing evidence that it's making a comeback. I included the word on a test for potential interns and was dismayed to see that only one applicant flagged it. Even worse, I've heard it used to mean college students in general, male and female. I guess that solves the sexism problem, but then there's the just-plain-wrong problem.

There's nothing wrong with *coeducational* or its shortened form as an adjective, but the noun *coed* is best reserved for irony and anachronism. And, I suppose, porn.

## COFFEE SHOP

This would have been a *tremendous* term for Starbucks and its ilk. Just outstanding. The trouble is, the term was already taken. It means something like a Denny's—a restaurant that keeps long hours, perhaps even staying open 24 hours a day, and offers breakfast even when it isn't breakfast time. A diner, but with carpeting. Starbucks is a *coffee bar* or something. See BUSH, GEORGE; FLASH MOB; and PHONE BOOK.

## COMPASS DIRECTIONS

Although it makes sense to capitalize *the West, the South* and so on as regions, the words should not be capitalized as directions. If you're in the North and you're traveling to the South, you're going *south*. Go *west*, young man. A closer call but also lowercase: *up north, back east, out west, down south*.

## COMPOUNDS AND DICTIONARIES

You've probably seen lists of commonly misspelled words before (perhaps in *The Elephants of Style?*), but perhaps a bigger problem, at least for reasonably educated writers armed with a dictionary, is a lack of awareness of the use, or non-use, of spaces and hyphens in the formation of compound words.

People confuse the issue of one word vs. two words vs. hyphenated words with the more contentious issue of hyphenating more-than-one-word modifiers, which I covered earlier. I've despaired about writers' and editors' ignorance of the basic principles of how and when to use reference materials to decide onewordization issues. With compound nouns, it's usually simple: You look in your house style manual, if you have one. If you find nothing there, you look in your house dictionary. If you find nothing there, and you're dealing with a noun, *stop*. Do not grab a different dictionary. Do not pass Go. Do not collect $200. *Make it two words*. If you're using Associated Press style, that dictionary is *Webster's New World*, Fourth College Edition. (Don't make the mistake of thinking all dictionaries with *Webster* in their names are the same. While the Merriam-Webster people are the legitimate heirs to the Noah Webster legacy, anybody can use the name—and the AP is using that other *Webster's*. And, for what it's worth, I find the *American Heritage Dictionary* most satisfying when I want to check on substance rather than spelling or orthography.)

With compound verbs, as with compound adjectives, you generally want a hyphen if the noun equivalent isn't already solid. Say you've cornered an intruder in your kitchen and grabbed a length of twine. You might need to consult your dictionary of choice to decide whether to *hog-tie* him or *hogtie* him, but you would never *hog tie* someone. Compound verbs, especially transitive ones, just don't work that way.

Compound nouns, as your dictionary will indicate, are more of a free-for-all. Why aren't they a *free for all* or a *freeforall*? Well, just because. The "everything always changes always, so just pretend it's a hundred years from now and shut up about it" crowd will blithely say that onewordization is the way of all flesh, but clearly that's not the case. Some very old and very common compound nouns have stubbornly kept their spaces or hyphens, which is the main reason I get so worked up over the tendency to obliterate spaces and hyphens in *Web site*, *e-mail* and the like. A paper clip is still a paper clip, and the reason isn't that paper clips are decidedly low-tech. The reason is that *paperclip* just doesn't look right. Kind of like *website* and *email*.

Some two-word forms (for now, at least) commonly misused as onewords: *back story*, *council member*, *cup holder*, *face time*, *flash point*, *game plan*, *grass roots* (n.), *grass-roots* (adj.), *head shot*, *home builder*, *home buyer*, *hot seat*, *jet stream*, *lock step*, *log in and log on* (v.), *log-in and log-on* (n., adj.), *pay stub*, *power broker*, *price point*, *prime time* (n.), *prime-time* (adj.), *rain forest*, *road map*, *road trip*, *rubber band*, *service member*, *slide show*, *sound bite*, *time slot*, *time stamp* (n.), *time-stamp* (v., adj.), *tip line*, *video game*. Trust me. I have an uncanny knack for this.

Some one-word forms commonly misused as two words: *barbershop*, *bookstore*, *drugstore*, *paycheck*, *nightclub*, *schoolteacher*, *sportswriter*, *stylebook*. If you love to look ignorant, one great way is to mix antique two-word forms with way-too-quickly-evolved onewordizations: *I took my pay check to the drug store to buy a cupholder, a videogame, and style books for school teachers and sports writers.* An e-mail or a letter or a thesis or an article or a book littered with questionable decisions on the onewordization front makes a statement that the writer probably would rather not make. That statement: "You're probably reading something produced by justin4326@aol.com, not by David Remnick and his team of professional editors."

We can disagree about some of my examples, of course, and I have my problems with the dictionaries as well as with amateurs. You'll find my Dictionary Dissents scattered throughout the book. *Webster's New World* would aim *cross hairs* at a *cabdriver* wearing a *sweat shirt* in his *town house*. (Other Dictionary Dissents point out some odd spelling choices. As in: *I must say, with tranquillity and largess, that seviche is on my shortlist of bootee accouterments.*)

The basic principles I'm outlining go out the window with certain colorful coinages, ones that often have a derogatory slant. Like *douchebag*, or the more recent variant *douchenozzle*. You won't find *stupidhead* in the dictionary, but that's what you were saying if, like me, you were fond of that term in second grade. It doesn't really refer to a head as being stupid, and so it's not "stupid head." The same goes for *graybeard* and *bluehair* as terms for the people who have gray beards and blue hair, as opposed to terms for said beards and said hair. *Asshat. Scumbucket. Turdblanket.* You get the picture.

## CONCERTED

To make a concerted effort is to make an effort in *concert* with others. It's not hard to understand why people hear the way "a concerted effort" is used and assume it means to try really, really hard, but there are plenty of other words for that.

## CONGRESS MEMBERS

This phrase is an ugly, ugly application of the "omit needless words" mantra. The expression is *members of Congress*. And keep in mind that the term covers the Senate as well as the House of Representatives, even though, confusingly enough, *congressmen* and *congresswomen* refer strictly to lawmakers in the House. (See REPRESENTATIVE.)

# COWORKER

As a copy editor and not a cop yeditor, I reserve this term for those who ork cows. My colleagues are *co-workers*.

# CUSTARD

It's a cooked milk-and-egg mixture eaten as a dessert or used as a base for other desserty things, such as sauces and ice cream. If you mean the variety of ice cream known as *frozen custard*, please say "frozen custard." That way the extreme cold won't shock my tongue. (Ditto for *yogurt* and *frozen yogurt*.)

# DECEPTIVELY

If a hill is *deceptively* steep, it's steeper—not less steep—than it looks.

# DEMONSTRATOR

Not *demonstrater*. Don't ask why; just memorize it. See PROTESTER.

# DIS

The now-almost-hoary slang term for "disrespect" is *dis*, not "diss." Don't be confused by the doubled *s* in *disses*, *dissed* and *dissing*.

Occasionally you'll read about a contact "lense" or a camera "lense" because of similar confusion: The plural of *lens* is *lenses*. Another such confusion, however, has resulted in a legitimate word—at least in English. *Tamales*, in Spanish, is the plural of *tamal*. English speakers, ignorant but hungry, saw all those *tamales* and invented the *tamale*. I would never dis either a tamal or a tamale, though I make no such promises on "potatoe" and "tomatoe."

## DMV

This appellation for the D.C. region—the District of Columbia, Maryland and Virginia—would have been perfect. Just great. The trouble is, it was already taken. Perhaps you've been to the Department, or Division, of Motor Vehicles? I'm tempted to suggest *DVM*, but I fear that would frighten my cats.

## DO

The restaurant industry operates on narrow margins even in the best times. In these recessionary times, cutbacks have to be made, and so words like *cook, prepare, order* and *eat* have been pink-slipped in favor of the very versatile verb *do*, which also retains its previous *do* meanings.

"I know the chef does a great grouper crudo with wasabi ice, but I think I'll do the sweetbreads with pumpkin and fall spices. Isn't it great that we can do a date night like this?"

(I'd make a bigger to-do about this, but I do it way too often myself.)

# DONDER

Apparently that's the reindeer's name, not *Donner*. I'm as surprised and, frankly, disappointed as you are. Perhaps a constitutional amendment to install the much more sensible Rankin-Bass spelling?

# DOUBLE POSSESSIVE

The double possessive is a matter of some controversy. Some insist that constructions like "a friend of Bill's" are redundant and therefore should be avoided. Others see "an old pal of mine" and extrapolate that, because you'd never say "an old pal of me," you also must reject "a friend of Bill."

I say trust your ear over either dogma. "A friend of Bill's" probably is better, except in the Clinton-era coinage,* but it's not a must. The following over-the-cliff application of the principle, which appeared in the *Washington Post*, illustrates one reason the double possessive has to be treated as optional, at least in some cases:

> Lanier has long been a favorite of Ramsey's, who gave her key patrol commands and later put her in charge of the bomb squad, SWAT team and other special units.

It was *Ramsey*, of course, not "Ramsey's" (Ramses?), who gave Lanier those responsibilities.

---

* This is getting to be ancient history, but in the 1990s it became fashionable to refer to those with connections, perhaps not readily apparent, to the 42nd president as *Friends of Bill*, or *FOBs*.

# DOWNFALL

It means ruin or the cause of that ruin. *A fondness for high-priced call girls was Spitzer's downfall*. It does not mean *drawback* or *downside*, as in "The lack of stainless-steel appliances and granite countertops in the house on Webster Street was a real downfall." Closer, but still wrong, is the meaning *setback*, as in "Jennifer Capriati was able to pull herself together after all those downfalls."

(I've also heard *killjoy* misused that way. Good Lord.)

# DOMESTIC

I pointed out in *The Elephants of Style* that Samuel Adams Boston Lager often shows up on bars' lists of "imported" beer. That phenomenon bubbled up at the tavern where the American Copy Editors Society toasted the conclusion of its 2010 conference in Philadelphia.

We were given wristbands that entitled us to $3 pints of domestic draft beer, and so I took a look at the taps and pointed to a Pennsylvania microbrew. That would cost more than $3, the bartender told me, adding that "'Domestic' means Bud, Miller, Coors . . ."

*Webster's New World* lists five definitions for domestic. Dictionaries being descriptivist and all, it might be time to add a sixth:

**6. ordinary or inexpensive [*domestic* beer]**

*Pedestrian* and *provincial* could also describe the mistaken definition, and I'm reminded of a time at my college newspaper at the University of Arizona when someone criticized a headline as "so *Citizen*." Neither the italics nor the capital C registered with my ears, and for a second that reference to one of the local dailies, the *Tucson Citizen*, registered as a perfectly reasonable adjective. You know, *citizen*, like *pedestrian*! If those two words have a once-removed familial relationship, *domestic* and *provincial* are more like first cousins. In other words, maybe it's the beer talking, but this error is looking more and more understandable to me.

By the way, I settled for a Yuengling, brewed in Pottsville, Pa., the town of my birth, which might qualify as premium elsewhere but is "domestic" in both senses of the word in Pennsylvania. (Is there a term that means "non-premium" but wouldn't turn off the marketing types? "Regular beer," to follow the gasoline analogy, falls a little short.)

## DOUBLE DOWN

In blackjack, doubling down is doubling one's bet after the initial deal—usually in response to being dealt a strong first two cards, seeing a weak card in the dealer's hand, or a combination of the two. A player who doubles down then gets one additional card and must play that hand, rather than having the option of taking more cards. The metaphor, therefore, should mean more than just an escalation. It should involve some element of additional risk. And maybe comped adult beverages.

## DOUBLE-WIDE

There was a time when this was amusing as sly synecdoche, a way of saying *mobile home* without saying "mobile home"; a way of getting across *trailer trash* without being so offensive about it. Now it's a cliche. Let's retire it.

223

# E-MAIL

I've voted against it, early and often, but *email* is well on its way to victory over *e-mail*. It's stupid that it's true, and I wish it weren't true, but it's true. AP style already omits the hyphen, and someday, maybe *to-morrow*, the more discerning style mavens will fall in line and that hyphen will be as quaint and old-fashioned as my aversion to tattoos on people who are neither longshoremen nor veterans of the Battle of Guadalcanal.

I don't plan to sign the truce any time soon, but when I eventually do, here's my demand: Please stop yawningly dismissing *email* as a routine example of the principle that compounds in English tend to evolve into solid forms. That tendency exists with actual word-plus-word compounds, but *e-mail* is not made up of two words. *E-mail* is a letter-plus-word compound, and letter-plus-word compounds have always kept their hyphens (or spaces, as the case may be). Repeat after me: *A-frame. B-movie. C-rations, D-Day.* And don't give me the speech about how *email* was inevitable because it's far more common than other such terms (do you take off your *tshirt* when you get an *xray*?).

So, yes, *email* is an example of the onewordization principle, but you must admit that it's an utterly exceptional one, a groundbreaker. It illustrates another idea: that there's a first time for everything.

# EPICENTER

I'm not as agitated about the non-seismic use of this word as some of my pickypants brethren seem to be. Yes, the earthquake term means the place *above* the center of the disturbance, but to me, if anything, that makes the metaphorical extension even more appropriate.

224

(We're living up here, after all, not on the way to the Earth's core.) I will, however, sign my colleagues' petitions if they want to make two points: 1. People do have an unfortunate tendency to misinterpret unfamiliar word beginnings as intensifiers. The epicenter must be the really, really center part! Penultimate must mean really, really ultimate! This house I'm trying to sell you isn't just in a perfect location; it's in a *pluperfect* location. 2. Vivid metaphors fade pretty quickly when they're overused. Not every center is an *epicenter*, not every large thing is *massive*, not every example of passive learning is *through osmosis* . . .

# EX-

Write *ex-French president*, not *French ex-president*. While it's tempting to try to steer clear of the "What, he's not French anymore?" parsing, down that road lies madness. There are tax ex-collectors, mail ex-carriers, beauty ex-queens and copy ex-editors. The sane thing to do is to treat *ex-* as a proxy for *former*. When possible, of course, you should just use *former*. This is an especially good idea when the abbreviation for Los Angeles International Airport comes into play.

# EXPOUND

*Expanding on* an idea and *expounding* (skip the *on*) an idea are similar. Basically, if you're laying something out, if you're introducing it, you're *expounding* it. If that something is already on the table, already introduced, you might *expand on* it by adding more details. The common trap here is reaching for the fancy word when the plain one is correct.

# FAMOUS

In addition to meaning "famous," *famous* is often used to indicate that something is a specialty, even when the idea of actual fame would be ridiculous.

> "I'm making my famous turkey-jalapeno chili tonight!"
> "I've never heard of it, but it sounds great! Should we get a six-pack of Sam Adams to go with it?"
> "Nah—it's pretty good even with domestic beer."

# FLASH MOB

This would have been an *outstanding* term for criminal activity carried out spontaneously by impromptu gangs of youth. Just tremendous. The trouble is, at the risk of repeating myself, the term was already taken. It means a gathering arranged through electronic communication, usually for the purpose of some sort of wacky performance art. I suppose criminal activity arranged through electronic communication would qualify, but seeing other people your own age and deciding to team up with them for beatings and robberies does not. See BUSH, GEORGE; COFFEE SHOP; and PHONE BOOK.

# FRANKENSTEIN

Yeah, yeah, yeah, it's the monster's creator, not the monster. But *Frankenstein's monster* has a clunky and pedantic feel that I'd rather avoid, and so if you're looking to make a Frankenstein reference you may want to do it obliquely, referring to *a Frankenstein situation* or some such so that you're suggesting the monster but retaining plausible deniability.

I thought of the creator-monster confusion when my *Washington Post*, of all newspapers, had to run a correction because it referred to Daniel Ellsberg as a psychiatrist. The phrase *Daniel Ellsberg's psychiatrist* was a Watergate-era staple, and it's easy to see how someone who lived through those days could, all these years later, distill it into a psychiatrist named Daniel Ellsberg.

## FREE

What it really means is "free of charge," and so it's an adjective, not a noun. If you say *for free*, you're turning it into a noun that means "nothing." So don't do that.

But there's a but. Sometimes you can't get rid of the darn *for*. Say you're Billy Joel in "Piano Man," or Liz Phair in "Polyester Bride," and you have this bar where you can drink for free. "Drink free" just doesn't sound quite right. So omit the *for* when you can, but—call it a nod to language change or an accommodation to comprehension—don't when you can't.

As an extra added bonus lagniappe, I'll also mention that the word is often redundant ad-speak, as in *free gift*.

## FUN

Speaking of nouns and adjectives, are you having a fun time?

No, you aren't. And not just because some past-his-prime newspaper guy is yelling at you. *Fun* in "We had fun" or "It was fun" is a noun. It's the *time* in "a good time," not the *good*. Because the *fun* in "It was fun" looks like an adjective—you'd say "It was pleasurable," not "It was pleasure"—the word has taken on the role of an adjective in informal usage.

Go ahead and say you're having a fun time (I do), but resist the urge to write it in anything more formal than an e-mail between friends. And remember: Free fun is better than fun-free.

## GAY MARRIAGE

That's almost always what you're talking about when you talk about *same-sex marriage*, but I lean toward that more precise term in legal contexts. A law allowing or forbidding the practice would apply even if no gay people were involved—there would be no exception for, say, two straight women tying the knot for green-card purposes. (Hyphen alert: *Gay-marriage supporters* are people, gay or straight, who support the idea of gay marriage. *Gay marriage supporters* might be homosexuals who enjoy pageantry and tiered cakes.)

## GIRLIE AND GIRLY

I haven't yet seen this distinction codified (dictionaries list both spellings as used for both meanings), but I think usage proves me right here: *Girly* is an adjective meaning *girlish*. If, ladies, you favor dresses and makeup and pigtails, you might be a girly girl. *Girlie* as a noun is a playful and possibly demeaning reference to a woman ("Hey there, girlie!"). The adjective *girlie* brings men into the equation—it denotes prurient interest, somewhere on the continuum between glamour and pornography. *Playboy* is a girlie magazine; *Seventeen* is a girly magazine. I found a reference online, in a woman's blog entry poking fun at her husband's subscription to *Men's Health*, to "men and their girly (not girlie) mags." Well played, madam. Well played.

So, then, what do you call a gentleman who eats quiche and drinks strawberry daiquiris and can't bench-press a can of coffee? The correct answer, of course, is whatever his name is, but play along with me for a second here and pretend you're a boorish lout. *Girly man* seems like an obvious answer at first glance, but a more nuanced analysis of Hans/Franz/Arnold has me thinking *girlie men*, perhaps with a hyphen. The intended meaning seems closer to *men who might as well be girlies* than to *men who are girlish*. Subtle, I know, but *Saturday Night Live* catch phrases and Austrian-born bodybuilders-turned-movie-stars-turned-U.S.-politicians can be that way.

## GOTCHA

Funny word, isn't it? Here I shall muse about it, in an entirely descriptive fashion, after using it to de-escalate one of those descriptive-vs.-prescriptive discussions that loosely form the theme of this book. If I say it to you directly, it's a friendly word—"ah, I understand" in the case of that discussion, or at worst a very playful way of saying "you just proved my point." Use it to describe someone else's actions, however, and it sounds more hostile. It's semi-playful in the "Gotcha Gang," as William Safire called readers fond of pointing out his errors, but in "gotcha journalism," for example, the word has a harsher edge. It's been used by descriptivists to, uh, describe the kind of scolding that people like me do.

# GRAB

This ugly word has become tech jargon for an image taken ("grabbed") from an electronic medium—a *screen grab* from a computer, or a *frame grab* from video or film. It's fine in conversation, but stick with the simple and elegant word *image* in actual writing.

# GRAND SLAM

In baseball, it's a home run with the bases loaded. In tennis and golf, it's winning the four major tournaments in the same calendar year. At Denny's, it's two eggs any style, two pancakes, two strips of bacon and two sausage links. (In bridge, it's something or other.) The baseball and bridge terms are lowercase; the tennis, golf and high-cholesterol-breakfast terms are uppercase.

In tennis, the term, sometimes abbreviated to *Slam*, is often casually used to refer to a championship at *any* of the four major tournaments, or simply to any of those tournaments themselves. That's fine in casual conversation, but in actual writing, one of those titles is *a Grand Slam title* and one of those tournaments is *a Grand Slam tournament.* You might hear that Rod Laver won two Grand Slams and also that Patrick Rafter won two Grand Slams, but those two Australians accomplished two very different things. Laver won the 1962 Australian championships, the 1962 French championships, the 1962 Wimbledon championships, the 1962 U.S. championships, the 1969 Australian Open, the 1969 French Open, the 1969 Wimbledon and the 1969 U.S. Open. (The various opens didn't become open—open to both amateurs and professionals—until 1968.) Rafter won the 1997 U.S. Open and the 1998 U.S. Open. That's it. Two Grand Slam *titles*. Two more than me, and nothing to sneeze at, but not two Grand Slams. To put that in Denny's terms, he ordered four eggs.

Laver, by the way, won a handful of major titles outside 1962 and 1969, for a total of 11. That's a lot of eggs.

## GRIDLOCK

The word isn't an all-purpose term for heavy vehicular traffic. It means a situation in which cars are stuck in intersections after their light has turned red, meaning that cars with the green light are also unable to move forward. The *grid* is *locked*. See how that works? Of course, that situation is never permanent or universal, and so there's some flexibility in how the term can be used, but there should be at least some element of true gridlock before it comes up.

## HABOOB

The dust flew a little in 2011 when many in Arizona got a little hot over the increasing use of this unfamiliar term for a familiar weather phenomenon—what I, who spent a decade in the desert, and others there knew of as a *dust storm*. The reaction took on a xenophobic flavor, and the "Don't use them Muslim words" outrage was another in a string of embarrassments for my former state. Although another word with Arabic origins, *monsoon*, has been commonly used in Arizona to describe another meteorological phenomenon since the 1950s, *haboob* was virtually unheard of among people who aren't meteorologists. Looking through its archives, the *Arizona Republic* found that a 1999 appearance of the term was the first since 1988. It appeared more frequently—gradually and then suddenly, as Hemingway might have said—after that. The term was new to me in 2011, as it apparently was to plenty of people in Arizona (I left in 1989). I deplore the bigotry, but I understand the puzzlement. Imagine going to sleep to the sound of thunder and waking to hear everybody on TV and radio talking about the "regensturms."

## HAIL

"Hail from Ohio" is, like haboobs, a weather phenomenon. Let's retire the cliche that tarts up a simple statement about a person's place of residence or birth.

## HANDOUT

A word that means alms for the poor or maybe a sheet of paper used to accompany a class or speech or lecture or seminar has been appropriated by professional photographers to mean an image not taken by them. That's fine—all professions have their slang (they also *make* photos rather than taking them)—but what's not fine is foisting this off on the public. A pic of the spiffy new '59 Bel Air provided by General Motors, like a shot of the latest serial killer provided by the Snohomish County Sheriff's Office, is not a "handout" when it comes time to write the credit line. GM PHOTO. PHOTO BY GM. PHOTO COURTESY OF GM. See how easy that was? This epidemic has progressed to the point where a picture doesn't actually have to be a "handout" to be a handout. The photo editors I work with see a photo taken by a freelancer rather than someone on their staff and stamp HANDOUT HANDOUT HANDOUT all over it. The word is apparently now code for *the other*. (Actually, there's no rubber-stamping anymore—they type the word in the electronic caption field, but you get the picture.)

## HOOP

Just when I thought nothing could surprise me anymore in the usage department, I heard a woman refer to her "hula hoop skirt." A quick Google check found a fair number of people using the term— something like a third of all references to hoop skirts. Sigh. Let's re- view: There are *hoop skirts*. There are *Hula Hoops*. It's possible that a whimsical type somewhere built a *Hula Hoop skirt*, but that's not the normal state of affairs. Such a garment would get kind of noisy. Note the capitalization: Hula Hoop is a registered trademark of Wham-O Inc., just like Frisbee and Hacky Sack. And there will be no "hoop- ing and hollering," except possibly in punny headlines about basket- ball or Wham-O products. The word you want there is *whooping*.

## INAUGURAL

In talking about a presidential inauguration, the adjective from *in- augural address* and *inaugural festivities/ceremony/events/whatever* is sometimes used as a noun. The usage can't really be called wrong, especially for the address, but discerning stylists will note that the proper terms are sitting right there. Washington gave his first inau- gural *address* at his first *inauguration*.

# INSTALL

You *install* microwave ovens. You *instill* a belief or a work ethic or a love of silly Dire Straits songs from the '80s.

# IS, IS

When I last checked, in writing *The Elephants of Style*, the state of the art was a doubling of the word. What started as "The problem is, I have a problem" became, pretty darn standardly, "The problem is, is I have a problem." Well, ladies and gentlemen, alert the Guinness people.

Thank you. Now that I have my beer, I'm going to try to set a world record. Here goes.

*The problem is, is: "Is" is "is." "Is" is not some other word.*

There you have it. Six. I need another beer.

# IZOD AND LACOSTE

Remember when preppy fashion was all the rage and everyone wore Izod alligator shirts? Yeah, well, you're wrong. Or at least misguided. Izod is technically correct, or at least it was, but to call a Lacoste shirt an Izod product is like referring to Coca-Cola by the name of your local bottling company (and here's a big Tucson shout-out to "The good guys at Kalil"!). Until the '90s, Izod had the U.S. contract to manufacture and distribute Lacoste shirts. Today, Lacoste shirts are just Lacoste shirts. (They're also polo shirts, if not Polo shirts.) Lacoste is Coke; Izod was, but is no longer, Kalil. Izod still makes shirts, but, alas, they are alligator-free.

As a matter of fact, all "alligator shirts," even the Lacoste ones, are alligator-free. That animal on preppies' chests is no gator. René Lacoste, the French tennis legend who founded the company, was nicknamed "Le Crocodile," and his nickname lives on on his shirts. So if you talk about "Izod alligator shirts," it's *really* a croc.

## JEW

The adjective is *Jewish*. To use *Jew* adjectivally, as in *Jew businesses* or *the Jew part of town*, is the mark of a bigot. Compare that to the way people who don't like Democrats make a point of saying *Democrat policies* rather than *Democratic policies*. There's also a verb form of *Jew* that's a slur.

The noun *Jew* is perfectly fine, though I once worked for an editor who considered it tainted, who insisted that it be changed to *Jewish person* because "'Jew' sounds offensive—you know, like 'dirty Jew'?" Um, well, maybe if you left out the "dirty" part?

## LAPTOP

Yes, everybody knows it means *laptop computer*. No, the word isn't used to mean the top of one's lap. Yes, the latter would be redundant anyway; a lap *is* a top. Still, just humor me and toss in the word *computer* at least once if you're using it in actual writing. See PICKUP.

## LECTERNS AND PODIUMS

For reasons I cannot fathom, my brethren in the picky-about-the-language biz consider this the biggest issue ever. Yes, a speaker stands *at* a lectern and *on* a podium. The thing with the seal of the president of the United States of America or the Grand Rapids Chamber of Commerce is a lectern; it may or may not be atop a podium or platform. Big deal, but all right—let it never be said that I crusaded against correctness. Now then: *Podium* is a word that people understand, even if they misunderstand it. Let me rephrase that: *Podium* won't distract readers; *lectern* just might. (You know what other word I'm just not comfortable with? *Nuance.*) So, assuming a podium was involved, I'd rather see *at the podium* changed to *on the podium* than to *at the lectern.* I'll get off my soapbox now.

## LIABLE AND LIBEL

The words sound similar, but any relationship between the two is purely tangential. If you hear that a publisher is canceling a tell-all book because of *liability* fears, or an editor says you can't repeat an accusation because you might be *liable*, you're hearing a case of mistaken identity, even if it isn't an outright error. The publication of false defamatory material with reckless disregard for the truth is *libel*. If a judge decides you committed libel and assesses a monetary judgment against you, then, sure, you're *liable* for that amount. But that liability would hold no matter what your original misdeed was—if you don't toss around the word *liable* when cautioning somebody to drive safely, you shouldn't toss it around when talking about defamation. If you want to explicitly refer to committing libel, say *committing libel.*

## LICENSE

A 16-year-old's exclamation of "I got my license!" is immediately understandable as meaning *driver's license*, but there are many kinds of licenses, so in writing it's a good idea to say exactly what you mean. To refer to your license without context tends to imply that you need a license to exist. Similarly, when I hear "What's your number?" I'm tempted to answer, "Uh, 5?" But I don't. Really, I'm not a big, fat jerk. I know it means telephone number, and I insist on having that spelled out only in actual writing. Oh, and my e-mail is . . . my e-mail. All those electronic messages I've received. If you mean my e-mail *address*, well, say that.

## LITE

The spelling makes sense to me when the meaning is a watered-down or dumbed-down version of something ("Walsh's books are like *linguistics lite*"). Confine the spelling to snark, though: Lite beer from Miller is still a *light* beer, as are Bud Light and all the others that, because of Miller's trademark, have to use the conventional spelling.

## LONG-STANDING, LONGTIME

One takes a hyphen, and the other does not. Don't ask why; just memorize.

## MAC AND CHEESE

In *Lapsing Into a Comma*, I wrote about *tux, limo, veggies* and *Lab* supplanting the actual words *tuxedo, limousine, vegetables* and *Labrador retriever*. Not railing against slang, mind you (that would be silly), but, well, railing against slang being treated as non-slang, I guess. Grown-ups would be well advised to use words such as "veggies" sparingly if at all. Anyway, allow me to add to that list *mac and cheese*. This comfort-food concept is so central to American life that it apparently demands a more easily spit-out-able moniker; heaven forbid anyone waste 1.5 seconds saying "aroni."

And then there's *baths*, as in "two bedrooms and 1½ baths." I have no problem with that as real-estate argot, but, for Pete's sake, maybe throw in the *-room* once every 10 times? I've even seen it migrating into the bedroom, leaving houses with "two *beds* and 1½ baths."

## MACY'S DAY

"The Macy's Day Parade" just kind of rolls off the tongue, but wait a minute: *Macy's Day?* When does *that* fall? And what would be an appropriate gift? The New York department store's Thanksgiving parade is, of course, *the Macy's Thanksgiving Day Parade*.

## MADAM

The word requires no additional feminization, so there's no need to tack on that distaff *e* and make it the French *madame*. You're free to address women, French and otherwise, as "Madame," but the correct word in all those references to Hillary Clinton as secretary of state and Nancy Pelosi as speaker of the House was *madam*: *Madam Secretary* and *Madam Speaker*, not "Madame Secretary" and "Madame Speaker." (Yes, the word can also refer to the female proprietor of a brothel. Whether you consider the political commentary that might be inferred from that unfortunate or hilarious, these things happen.)

## MASSIVE

Have you noticed that everything these days is massive? Spending bills, earthquakes, opportunities—and, of course, heart attacks.

Now, I'm not going to insist that the word be limited to things that have great mass. That would be denying you *tons of fun*. But I am tired of the cliche. "I just ate a *massive* hot-fudge sundae" is a pretty hyperbolic thing to say—how truly massive could a sundae be?—and as such it once would have drawn a smile. Through overuse, the metaphoric usage has become standard, rote, ordinary.

Come to think of it, I suppose that's why we have *ginormous*.

## MIDDLE AMERICA

You don't hear the term as often as you did during the Nixon administration, so the youngsters can be forgiven for thinking it means the Midwest, or maybe the region in the geographical center of the lower 48. The actual meaning is closer to what we now call *the red states*—it's a cultural observation about conservatism and conventionality that, yes, does tend to overlap with the region in question. But primarily it's a state of mind: An archetype for Middle America is Archie Bunker, the *All in the Family* antihero who lived in the very blue city of New York. (My dictionary tells me that the term does also have a geographical meaning, but that meaning is Mexico, Central America and sometimes the West Indies. If you've ever heard the term used that way, you probably count me among "the youngsters.")

# MIKE

In March 2010, I received this stylebook update by e-mail from the Associated Press:

> **mike** (n.) Shortened form of *microphone*. *Microphone* preferred on first reference. Use *miked, miking* as the verb forms.

Not long afterward, the entry was changed to this:

> **mic** (n.) Informal form of *microphone*.

As the editors of the stylebook explained (I am not making this up), the AP's broadcast people were outraged at the original entry and started feverishly pointing to the letters etched into their tape recorders next to the microphone jack. The editors reversed their ruling.

Note that there's no guidance on the verb forms. If I'm wearing one of them there "mics," am I "miced"? "Micced"? "Mic'd"? I asked the editors about that, and, sure enough, if a "mic" is strapped to me, in AP style, I'm "miked" by people who are "miking" me. Come to think of it, I forgot to ask about the present-tense verb. The entry does say "(n.)."

Now then: While there are no doubt many broadcast journalists who are gifted writers and spellers, that's not their forte. Many of them are in a non-print medium for a reason. Those of us who have more experience with the printed word know better than to take our cues from the abbreviations squeezed into limited space on electronic equipment; it's why we don't refer to volume controls as "vols."

Shortened forms tend to adopt phonetic spellings if a simple truncation would suggest an incorrect pronunciation. A refrigerator is a *fridge*, not a "frig." When a young Jennifer Capriati referred to Martina Navratilova as a legend but used only the first syllable of that word, she was calling her a *ledge*, not a "leg." (Perhaps Martina was always her fave! Yes, not *fav.*) Would a handkerchief be a "handke"? No. It's a hankie.

And a microphone is a *mike* (pronounced "mike"), just as a Michael is a *Mike*. Mickey? Sure, make him *Mick*.

## MISPLACED

Now, where did I put that definition? It means, of course, put in the wrong place (as in a misplaced modifier), and often lost, as least temporarily, as a result (as in your damn car keys more often than you'd like to remember). I thought everybody knew that, but one evening I was watching one of my house-hunting programs on TV and one of the potential buyers mentioned that his family runs a business that helps "people misplaced from their homes." I laughed, and my Twitter followers laughed, and then the next day I searched the Web for the phrase. It turns out more people are misplaced from their homes than I thought. Google found more than 7,000 examples of the usage. My faith in copy editing was restored when LexisNexis found just one occurrence in an actual newspaper. For the record: People are *displaced* from their homes.

# MOIST

Yes, I know how much you hate that word. So stop talking about it already.

# MORAYS

A more (pronounced "moray") is a societal norm. A moray (pronounced "moray") is a kind of eel. Occasionally the two are confused. Politico.com:

> "In one decade, what's shocking on TV is accepted as commonplace in the other," said Rep. Jack Kingston (R-Ga.), a veteran of the culture wars of the 1990s. "It's the same with sexual mores all over that if you look at campuses and universities, they have a lot of gay pride clubs and so there has been a deliberate and effective outreach to the younger generation about being more accepting of same-sex relationships."

*Sunday News*, Lancaster, Pa.:

> Literary icon Joyce Carol Oates offered wry asides on sexual morays in the '50s while reading from her latest novel, *The Falls*.

*Shreveport Times:*

> A newly elected tea party Republican senator recently stated that "Many Republicans treat war like Democrats treat welfare," shedding light on a glaring deficiency in conservative critique of the states' growth. While they are spot on in analyzing federal

welfare's potential to erode social morays, this suspicion is absent when it comes to the claims government makes about war and foreign policy.

*Toronto Star:*

> This was a crime of extreme passion," said Dyson.
> "Doubtless religious and cultural morays played a large part. It does not in any way justify or permit a violent attack on anyone for cultural and religious beliefs."

## MOSTEST

That would be the super-superlative, if you're reaching for one for comic effect, as in *hostess with the mostest*. "Hostess with the mostess" had never even occurred to me when I came across it while writing this book. I was floored to see that it outnumbers the logical version by 2 to 1 online. *Mostest* has a slight edge in a LexisNexis search, where the content is more likely to have been edited, and an edge approaching 4 to 1 when that search is narrowed to "major newspapers." That makes sense, because "mostess" doesn't. Pronounce it that way if you like, but you don't get to alter a spelling to make your rhyme look better than it is, no matter how many people give you a "sneak peak." (*You're a poet and don't even noet!*)

## MOTLEY

The word means diverse, varied, many-hued, possibly to the point of incongruity. That's it. It does not imply disrepute, though fans of the diverse, varied, many-hued, incongruous field of Republican presidential candidates in 2012 sure thought it did, judging from the reaction to my use of the word to describe the contenders in a head-line. I blame Vince Neil.

## NEWS CONFERENCES AND PRESS CONFERENCES

Some editors enforce the former, reasoning that television and radio (and now online) news outlets are not part of the *press*. How about we stop it already? The number of people who were alive the last time such a gaggle was limited to print reporters is dwindling fast, and it seems clear that press conferences and press releases will out-live that narrowly defined press. If we're still talking about "dialing" and "ringing" with telephones, surely we can consider all those non-ink-stained people with *press passes* part of the press.

## NIAGRA

Now, 'that's a spelling boner. The falls are *Niagara*, which served as an inspiration for the name of the drug *Viagra*, in combination with, it is said, *virility*, though *vital* and *vitality* also come to mind.

## NO PARTICULAR ORDER

I see this a lot in end-of-the-year top-10 lists, and it gets rather tire-some. If the list is *truly* in no particular order, then present it alpha-betically or chronologically or something. No, you say, Mr. and Ms.

Critic? Just as I thought. There *is* an order; you just don't want to take responsibility for it. It's a cop-out. And a put-on. Put-on! (The Who's "Eminence Front" was my 47th-favorite song of 1982.)

## NOD

When I read "nodding her head 'no,'" I shake my head. If you *nod*, of course your head is involved, and it means yes. If you *shake your head*, it means no. Got that? Hope you're nodding.

## ON

The word comes in handy sometimes. If you're covering the Neighborhood of Make-Believe, you might interview Sara Saturday. In the real world, you're more likely to be talking to Sara *on* Saturday.

## ONE OF THE ONLY

I'm one of the only language peevers who don't mind *one of the only*. Many object that the correct phrase is *one of the few*, because *only*, like *unique*, describes something that stands alone. If that's the case, though, are we to ban "Only two people showed up?" A more reasoned objection to the idea that *one of the only* is a perfectly good way of saying *one of the few* is that *only* can mean quite a bit more than a few. Maybe "only" a million people voted for a third-party presidential candidate (everything's relative), or "only" four out of five dentists surveyed recommend sugarless gum for their patients who chew gum (what's the deal with the other 20 percent?). Whereas *one of the few* at least narrows things down a little, the argument goes, *one of the only* could mean only two, or three or thousands. Fair point, but I think context will guide both the writer and the reader away from serious ambiguity. And it's not as though *one of the few* couldn't mean one out of tens of thousands, as in "He's one of the few dentists who recommend that their patients chew sugary gum." Would you also ban *one of the biggest* and *one of the smallest* and *one of the fastest* and *one of the slowest* and so on?

## OPPORTUNITY

See CHANCE.

## PADDLE BOATS

Yes, I suppose there's a paddle in the mechanism. But when you're talking about a swan-shaped thing you rent for a spin around the reservoir, as opposed to an olde-tyme Mississippi River steamer featuring gambling and extravagant headwear, don't you mean *pedal boats*?

## PERCENT

In addition to the usual problems with percentages (remember: a rate that went from 20 percent to 10 percent fell by 50 percent, or 10 *percentage points*, not 10 percent), Occupy Wall Street and its kin have given us new terms to trip over. "We are the 99 percent" has been a rallying cry, meaning that the richest 1 percent of the population should not wield outsize power. Although "the 1 percent" and "the 99 percent" are largely metaphorical, references to percentages still have to obey the laws of mathematics. So keep in mind that it makes no sense to refer to, say, the 2 or 3 percent as opposed to the 99 percent, because some people would belong to both groups. And beware of references to even-more-elite groups as distinct from the 1 percent. By definition, the top 0.1 percent and the 0.001 percent and the 0.0001 percent and so on are part of the top 1 percent.

## PHONE BOOK

This would be a great term for the little black book, the pocket-size personal directory of contact information for people in your life. Just perfect. The trouble is, the term is already taken. It means the public directory of telephone numbers—the white pages, yellow pages and blue pages. That very thick (at least in big cities) volume that muscle-men make a show of being able to rip in two. What the youngsters mean when they say "phone book" is an *address book*. (Youngsters also store their phone numbers in their cellphones, so I don't know why they're even talking about address books in the first place. Oh, and what do most cellphones call their directory features? Yep. "Address book.") See BUSH, GEORGE; COFFEE SHOP; and FLASH MOB.

## PICKUP

Yes, it can mean *pickup truck*, and using *pickup* alone to mean such a truck is fine in the right context. But don't go reverse-engineering a style ruling and take that dictionary entry to mean that *pickup truck* is somehow wrong or redundant or wordy or otherwise inadvisable. Even if there's no possibility that a reference to a pickup will be taken to mean the wanton trollop and all-around wonderful, wonderful new friend who accompanied you back to your motel room on a certain night to remember, the full term has a nice . . . *fullness* to it. You'll sound less like a person who drives one. (Joking. Joking! Some of my best friends drive pickup trucks! Heck, most of them do, for some reason. Yes, I'm an elitist. I thought we had already established that.) See LAPTOP.

## PORN AND PORNO

The adult thing to call adult material is *porn*. Twelve-year-old boys salivate over *porno* (or, even worse, *a porno*, as in *a* pornographic movie). You, assuming you're older than 12, enjoy *porn*. Well, at least I do. (I'm told by a reliable source that Larry Flynt detests the word *porno* and banned it from *Hustler* magazine.)

## POSSESSIVES THAT AREN'T

BIG BANG THEORY (ABC, 9 p.m.): Sheldon is unnerved by his mother's (Laurie Metcalf) visit.

No. The actress playing Sheldon's mother is Laurie Metcalf, not "Laurie Metcalf's." Write around it.

Sen. Edward M. Kennedy's (D-Mass.) bill was passed.

No. The Massachusetts Democrat in question was Edward M. Kennedy, not "Edward M. Kennedy's." Write around it.

*She dressed like "Gone With the Wind's" Scarlett.*

No. You know why. Write around the possessive if your style calls for quotation marks, or persuade your style guru to switch to italics and remember to hit ctrl/i again before you get to the apostrophe.

# PRIMARY

The word, when used to mean *primary election*, means *primary election*. What it does not mean is a series of primary elections. When I was working on this book, we were waiting to see who would emerge from the 2012 Republican presidential *primaries*, not "primary." In presidential races, they usually hold more than one. I need to write a blog about this on my blog.

# PROFESSOR

Someone is *a* professor or *the* professor. "She is professor of English at Harvard University"? You are Tonto of *Lone Ranger.*

# PROM

You go to *the* prom or *a* prom. Please stop talking about "going to prom." (And please, if I may offer some off-topic personal advice, don't go to *the* prom with *a* professor.)

## PROTESTER

Not *protestor*. Don't ask why; just memorize it. See DEMONSTRATOR.

## QUALITY

Some of my fellow pickypoos object to the use of *quality* as an adjective meaning high-quality, but I don't see the problem. (You wouldn't stop and think, oh, wait, do you mean *low*-quality?)

## RAMEN NOODLES

Okay, fine, you ate them in college because they're cheap and you were poor. Do they really need to be everyone's go-to metaphor for poverty? Let's retire the cliche.

## REARED

If you're still changing "raised" to "reared" when it involves people rather than animals, cut it out. People can be raised. I know I was. (If I was reared, it was done discreetly while I was sleeping.)

## RENOWN

I covered this in *Lapsing Into a Comma*, but perhaps not as clearly as I could have. *Renown* is a noun meaning fame and good reputation, and *renowned* is the adjective: A person with renown around the world is *world-renowned*. Perhaps because being renowned involves being known, that *k* has a tendency to creep in, so you sometimes see *reknowned*. And, perhaps because *known* is a past participle, people often think there's no need for the *-ed* with *renowned*, hence all the "world-renown" and "world-reknown" people you'll find on the Internet.

## REPOIRE

An amazingly large number of people think this is how to spell *rapport*. It's actually not a word at all, at least in English, though I suppose it could mean "pear again" in French. (You'll also see *report* used to mean rapport fairly often.)

## REPRESENTATIVE

It's the title given to those in the U.S. House of Representatives, but its status as a plain old generic word can lead to confusion. Even "your representatives in Congress" is ambiguous, because it could be seen as including the ones in the Senate. Use the title without fear when it's stylistically appropriate to capitalize or abbreviate it, but consider *congressman* or *congresswoman* instead of a lowercased *representative*. Everyone knows that congressmen and congresswomen are in the House, whereas the phrase *members of Congress* refers to members of the Senate as well, right? Oh. Well, there's always *House member*. (See CONGRESS MEMBERS.) With state legislatures, you're kind of stuck. There are no "state congressmen."

## THE RESERVES

In references to auxiliary military forces, the plural works as a reference to more than one reserve or as a casual reference to any of them: To be in the Army Reserve is to be *in the reserves* the same way that playing under the banner of Major League Baseball is playing *in the major leagues*. In less-casual references, however, each of the reserves is singular: *the Army Reserve, the Navy Reserve, the Air Force Reserve, the Coast Guard Reserve.*

## RESIGNING AND RETIRING

Speaking of members of Congress, how is it that we can see a headline saying they've retired and then see them doing all their lawmaking and filibustering and whatever else they do (sexting?) one month and two months and six months later? Answer: bad headline writers. To *retire* is to, um, retire. Saying you will be retiring at a later date—as in telling reporters in January that you're not going to seek re-election in November—is not retiring. If it were, I would have retired many times by now, because I've been saying since my 20s that once I hit 59½, I'm out of here.

Now, *resigning*, to me, is a different thing. If an official announces that she resigns, effective next week, the headline could legitimately say that she resigned. Sure, *announces her resignation* would be a little better, but the resignation is in the declaration. It's possible to keep performing your duties after you resign—just ask George Costanza.

While I'm in the *re-* column, a little *re*minder: Use a hyphen when you're *re-signing* a document or a star player on your NFL team, or re-tiring your 1972 Ford Pinto. Creating again is not recreation. Unless you're really into it, of course.

## RIDDLED

If a car gets shot up real good, it's bullet-*riddled*. You'll sometimes see "bullet-ridden," but that would be more appropriate to describe something weighed down by bullets, bullets more likely to have been dropped than fired. "Oh, dear, I've spilled an entire box of your father's hollow-point ammo in the pudding. Just *look* at all those bullets."

## ROUNDING

Yes, I know you were promised there would be no math. I'll make it quick. If the Dow Jones Industrial Average fell 2.46 percent and your publication's style is to use only one decimal place in such reporting, do you just lop off that last number? Of course not. If it's 4 or below, yes, you simply drop the digit; if it's 5 or above, you drop the digit and bump up the one that's left. So 2.44 is 2.4, but 2.46 is 2.5. And 2.45 is also 2.5, right? Well, yes and no. It is if 2.45 is truly what you're looking at, but that's not always the case. Maybe 2.45 is *already* rounded. Maybe whoever reported the percentage change in the first place uses two decimal places and the actual percentage change was 2.445 or 2.446 or 2.449. Those numbers round to 2.45 if you're using two decimal places but 2.4 if you're using one. So make sure you're working with raw numbers before you start rounding, and be aware that sets of figures that don't seem to add up might be just fine, only rounded.

Oh, and never round down to zero. Even if your style is one decimal place, 0.001 is 0.001. Your style can't be to say that nothing happened when something did, in fact, happen.

## ROUNDING ERROR

Speaking of rounding, it has become fashionable, especially in opinion writing, to refer to an amount that the writer considers insignificant as a *rounding error*. As in, the difference is no more important than if someone had gone up instead of down, or down instead of up, in rounding that last digit. Cliches spread fast in the Internet era, and this is a good example. Use it if you must, but be aware that it stopped being clever and original a while back.

## SANTE FE

The city in New Mexico (and those in Argentina and elsewhere) is, of course, *Santa Fe*. But the typist corner of our brains is always thinking ahead, and thus we get reverse-echo letter-anticipation typos. I mentioned "Saudia Arabia" and "American Online" in *Lapsing Into a Comma*, and my Twitter friends added "Forth Worth" and "Cape Code" to the list. If enough people commit those mistakes, do we have to change the names? (Also: Just try typing "Olive Garden" without making it "Oliver Garden" seven or eight times.)

## SEGWAY

I got a lesson in humility as I was preparing to lecture the youngsters about how the trademark for those funny motorized conveyances is a play on a generic word and not a generic word itself. All that is true, but I thought the word was *segueway*, a longer way of saying *segue*. In fact, as I learned way too late in life, *segue* itself is pronounced like *Segway*. I saw "segueway" in a 1977 book of *Saturday Night Live* scripts, and it made perfect sense. *Segue* would rhyme with *egg*, with its *-gue* behaving like the ones in *vague* and *vogue* and *league* and *fatigue*, and *segueway* would be "SEGG-way." As it turns out, however, *segueway* is an unnecessary variant, an attempt by those of us who didn't know the pronunciation of *segue* to create that pronunciation, just as *irregardless* is an attempt by those who don't process the negation in *regardless* to put it there. That'll teach me not to be such a pedagog-way.

## SERVICE LINE

Tennis, anyone? Next time you're watching Wimbledon or the U.S. Open or the Regions Morgan Keegan Championships and you hear the guy on TV talk about a player stepping up to the service line to start a point . . . yell "Foot fault!" Because that's what it would be if someone served from the service line, given that it's 18 feet into the court. The service line marks the back of the service box, which is where the serve has to land. The *baseline* is the line that players must stand behind when serving.

## SHEPARD

To *shepard* a plan is to take it on a fifteen-minute suborbital flight while sporting a jaunty crew cut. You probably mean *shepherd*.

# SHOOTING

What if they held a shooting and nobody got shot? Then it's not a shooting, I say. Others disagree. My own newspaper used the word regularly in coverage of the case of a guy accused of firing gunshots at buildings. But think about it: If I tell you there was a shooting at your office, your response is likely to be "Oh, no! Who got shot?" If somebody fires a gun at a person and misses, or fires a gun at something other than a person and hits that something, that person is a *shooter*, and *shooting* (v.) occurred, but *a shooting* (n.) did not.

# SHOWSTOPPER

A *showstopper* is something impressive, spectacular, awesome, as in a musical number in a play that brings audience members to their feet in applause, thereby stopping the show for a bit. In yet another sign that the theater may be dead, people are using the term to mean something like *dealbreaker*—an event that breaks off negotiations or otherwise pre-empts matters.

# SO WHAT?

A comma can be a good thing. Observe:

> *So what if I accidentally killed him?*
> *So, what if I accidentally killed him?*

## SODA

Maybe it's because I grew up in Michigan, where *pop* was a soft drink and *a soda* was an ice-cream soda. Maybe it's because it sounds more like plain seltzer than it does the heavily promoted multibillion-dollar sugar feast that's making the world fat. Go ahead and use whichever term is regionally correct for your novel or blog post, but neither *soda* nor *pop* seems appropriate as the standard term for a grown-up publication. *Soft drink* is a bit clunky, especially when *carbonated* might be necessary to make it clear you're not talking about orange juice or something, but I think it's a better choice. (If you're one of those "What kind of coke would you like, Pepsi or Sprite?" people, meet me in Chapter 14.)

## SOONER THAN LATER

Why, yes, it is! I know because I typed the phrase into an Excel spreadsheet and the cell returned "TRUE." Anyway, I think what people mean is "sooner *rather* than later."

## SPEED BUMPS AND SPEED HUMPS

Some people think the latter is a fancy new term for the former, but they're not the same thing. A speed bump is like a steep little hill, intended to slow vehicles to a near-stop in a parking lot, a garage or another place where the speed limit is extremely low. The speed *hump*—a more recent development—is broader and gentler, sometimes even a little plateau, intended to keep vehicles from speeding down a residential street. A car doing 15 mph would be jarred by a speed bump but would negotiate a speed hump just fine.

## SPIKING AND TANKING

Round about the turn of the 21st century, prices and other closely watched numbers stopped *rising* and *falling* and started *spiking* and *tanking*. If I ask nicely, will you consider giving those words a rest?

I suppose the meaning of *tanking* is clear enough, though it always takes my pea brain a couple of seconds to work through the metaphor and picture a *tank* as an olde-tyme swimming pool. From there, the mustachioed gentleman in his tight-fitting but limb-covering horizontally striped two-piece bathing costume taking a dive materializes pretty quickly and I get it—oh, right, *dive*.

*Spiking* is another matter. Maybe it's because I'm an olde-tyme newspaper type, but when I hear "spike," the first image that comes to mind is the pointy desk accessory on which editors impaled sheets of copy paper when a story was being discarded, killed, *spiked*. That was before my tyme (I'm not *that* olde), but my first couple of newsrooms retained a spike or two for ironic decorative purposes, and the verb *spike* still means to kill a story. The second image that comes to mind is a football player *spiking* the ball after a touchdown. To review: *Down* goes the story, *down* goes the football. There is that third image, of a fever chart and a pointy upward *spike*, and of course that's what the metaphor gods had in mind, but I think they dropped the ball on this one. I can't be the only one who hears "spike" and thinks downward thoughts, or at least confused ones. And is that image even representative? It's fine for a temporary sharp rise, but if a company's stock price shoots up *and stays there*, that doesn't paint such a pointy picture. It's more of a mesa, a butte, a . . . *plateau.* Oops. Tune in tomorrow for *When Metaphors Collide.*

## STATE ABBREVIATIONS

Occasionally we old-fashioned types are asked what the heck the deal is with this *Calif., Fla., Mich.* business. Why don't we use the modern, streamlined, newfangled state abbreviations provided to us by the U.S. Postal Service?

I usually don't like to answer a question with a question, but— quick—what's MI? Minnesota? Wrong. What's AK? Arkansas? Wrong! What's MS? Massachusetts? Wrong!

Yeah, I know you didn't get any of those wrong, because my readers are sharper than that, but trust me: Ordinary people outside of Arkansas and Alaska (I'll let you fill in your own redundancy joke) would bat maybe .600 on the AK question. People outside the United States would probably be stumped. And just as AK could be Alaska or Arkansas, AL could be Alabama or Alaska; MA could be Massachusetts or Maryland; MI could be Michigan, Minnesota, Mississippi or Missouri; MO could be Missouri or Montana; MS could be Mississippi or Missouri; and NE could be Nebraska or Nevada. I think that about covers it. Now, how many of the standard old-fashioned abbreviations used in Associated Press style run the risk of confusing people? *Miss.* and *Mo.* are the only ones that come to mind.

There's also the matter of the postal abbreviations looking ugly and unprofessional, but I suppose that's a matter of taste. There are those who think I'm ugly and unprofessional.

## STRONG SWIMMERS

Good swimmers aren't *good*; they're always *strong*. Nobody knows why.

## TARMAC

Some object to the use of the word to refer to the part of the airport where planes rest near the runways but not actually on the runways, on the grounds that they're no longer surfaced with *tar* and *macadam*. But the word is well established, and there's no other good term for it, so use it with my blessing. Have a safe flight.

## TAX RETURN

That's the form you fill out and send to the IRS. The check you might receive if you paid more than you owed is a tax *refund*.

## TEH

Irony alert: This common typographical error, as you know if you read a lot of Internet discourse (please skip ahead if you do, because I'm about to waste your time), has metastasized into its own creature. It's a device that's used to obliquely make fun of people whom the writer considers ignorant (and therefore more likely than most to commit such a typo), and so you might see a liberal blogger mock conservative attitudes about homosexuality by referring to *teh gays*. So, if you're an editor, take note. I'm not endorsing, just informing.

# TERROR

The primary meaning is intense fear, not terrorism. A reference to terror on a roller coaster should bring to mind white knuckles in good fun, not an Al Qaeda booby trap. Use *terror* if you must as a headline shortcut for all that unpleasantness, but spend a few extra letters and say *terrorism* and *terrorist* when that's what you're talking about. "War on terror" is fine if you're quoting the George W. Bush administration, but otherwise the term is best avoided.

# THEN-

The hyphen is needed only with a title used directly before a name: *Then-Mayor Monte Geralds.* Skip it when the title is used in apposition: *Monte Geralds, then mayor of Madison Heights, dedicated the building.*

# TITLES AND ARTICLES

I've long seethed over the exploitation of *a* and *the* by writers who force the words to do double duty. When I was hired by *The Phoenix Gazette*, I should have been welcomed to the *Gazette* staff, not *The Gazette* staff. That *the* goes with *staff*, not with *Gazette*, and thus should be lowercase. The capital letter would be appropriate with a possessive construction: *The Gazette's* staff.

The error is probably a symptom of the misapprehension that articles at the beginning of proper nouns can never, ever be dropped. As Strunk and White correctly pointed out, dropping them is quite all right.

WRONG: "You're a regular Daisy Buchanan," he said, referring to *The Great Gatsby* character. (It's the *Great Gatsby* character, like the *Gazette* staff.)

SILLY: She wore flapper dresses, like a *The Great Gatsby* character. (Just drop the The.)

FINE: He was a rich man, a guy right out of Fitzgerald's *The Great Gatsby*.

ALSO FINE: He was a rich man, a guy right out of Fitzgerald's *Great Gatsby*.

# TRAGEDY

Forgive me if I sound insensitive here, but a two-car crash that leaves three people dead is not a *tragedy*. Let the local-TV-news people have their hyperbole, but careful users of the language will reserve the word for bigger things. There doesn't necessarily have to be a hero and a flaw and all, but I at least want to start to think about reaching for the Greek mask when I see the term.

# TROVE

Strictly speaking, the word works only when it's paired with *treasure*. It's an Old French adjective meaning "found," and so a *treasure trove* (or *treasure-trove*, if you buy some American dictionaries' odd nod to British hyphenation) is a treasure found.

That French adjective is pretty well established as an English noun by now, though, so I say go ahead and use it. Just keep in mind that some will bristle.

## TURNED

Pick your style on *nun turned porn star* vs. *nun-turned-porn star* vs. *nun-turned-porn-star*, but please don't say *former nun turned porn star*, with or without hyphens. The *turned* part takes care of the *former* part.

## UNDOUBTEDLY

Is it just me, or is this word taking its place alongside *literally* as an "I mean the exact opposite of what I say" intensifier? As in this example that I'm totally making up:

> Jane Austen was undoubtedly thinking of the Houston Astrodome when she wrote, "To sit in the shade on a fine day, and look upon verdure is the most perfect refreshment."

To which the correct response would be: No, she wasn't.

## UNPAID

A sign at Target warned me not to bring "unpaid merchandise" into the restroom. So, I guess I should have paid the merchandise? Someone or something can't be unpaid if he, she or it couldn't have been paid in the first place. A bill can be paid, so you might have *an unpaid bill*, but "an unpaid meal," like "unpaid merchandise," makes no sense. You pay *for* the meal, so it's *an un-paid-for meal*. (Note the extra hyphen. The *un-* goes with the entire phrase, so you need to divorce it from *paid*.)

# UNTRACKED

Many athletes and athletic supporters have been hearing "on track" all their lives and thinking it was "untracked." So they say things like "The Redskins just couldn't get untracked out there today." I suppose they think "tracked" means "stuck in a rut"? That does make a certain amount of sense, come to think of it. As I mentioned in Chapter 6, the mistake has been around longer than sticklers might think.

# U.S. ATTORNEYS

Late in 2006, the George W. Bush administration's Justice Department fired nine people who held the title *U.S. attorney*. In headlines, second references and TV blather, the nine were often referred to as *attorneys*.

No.

OK, well, yes, they *were* attorneys, if you accept the term as a tarted-up synonym for *lawyers*, but to use it as an all-purpose shorthand for *U.S. attorneys* makes about as much sense as using it to describe Supreme Court justices.

The generic term for those who hold the title U.S. attorney is *federal prosecutor*, or simply *prosecutor*. In fact, it's a good idea to work *prosecutor* into any story on the matter even if *U.S. attorney* isn't too long to fit in a headline or too frequently mentioned as to become monotonous: There are bound to be people out there without a firm grasp of what exactly a U.S. attorney is. After all, if the title didn't exist, it's a construction that people might well use in place of *American lawyer*.

This is probably a good time to bring up a general principle about capitalization, because the word *attorney* seems to make people forget it: In general, titles get capital letters only when they're used as titles immediately before a name. *President Rutherford B. Hayes* was the *president*, not the *President*. Some publications are more promiscuous with their caps, but that's the way most do it. Why not make an exception for *U.S. attorney* to differentiate it from *American lawyer*? Well, just because. We do other things in the name of eliminating ambiguity, but that just isn't one of them. So while either *U.S. Attorney's Office* or *U.S. attorney's office* would be acceptable, depending on whether you want to capitalize such administrative divisions, *U.S. Attorney's office* is a mistake, as is *Attorney General's office* and *Sheriff's office*.

# USED TO

I used to ride my bike without a helmet. You didn't? Then you didn't *use* to, not "didn't used to." If you're an educated speaker (and I know you are), you might be particularly repelled by this reality, because you're used to reprimanding the riffraff for mimicking the common pronunciation of *used to* and dropping that *d* when writing the phrase. But hold your nose for a second and remember that education of yours and think about how helping verbs work. Observe:

"I had to go to the party."
"No, you didn't have to go [not *you didn't had to go*] to that party."

"I used all the toothpaste."

"No you didn't use it all [not *you didn't used it all*]—there's another tube in the medicine cabinet."

Another point on *used to*: Watch out for redundancy. The construction shouldn't be used if you've already established a time frame.

NO: *Back when LBJ was president, I used to ride my bike without a helmet.*

YES: *Back when LBJ was president, I rode my bike without a helmet.*

## VOICE MAIL

Yes, two words, but that's not my point. I came across a reference in a wire-service story to the reporter trying to contact a person mentioned, and it quoted "a message left on her voice mail." Rupert Murdoch and *News of the World* got into a lot of trouble for listening to messages on other people's voice mail, and I think in this case what the writer meant was the *greeting* on the voice mail. You record a *greeting*, and other people leave you *messages*.

## WAL-MART

The retailing giant that goes by that name decided at one point to redesign its logo and rebrand part of the company, and so its stores became *Walmart*. As with Exxon Mobil's ExxonMobil gas stations and J.C. Penney's JCPenney stores, that kind of silliness puts writers and editors in an awkward position. Observe the distinction and look silly, or ignore it and look pigheaded? Call me a pighead, but I think the lesser of evils is to pick the broader name and stick with it. If Wal-Mart runs Walmart stores, then they're also Wal-Mart stores. If the company doesn't like it, it's free to choose one name and not two virtually identical ones.

## WELCOME AND WELCOMED

The latter is often used when the former would do nicely. You may indeed be welcomed when you visit somebody, but the open invitation that prompts that visit should say you're *welcome*, not "welcomed," to drop by. (Then again, there are plenty of places where you'd be welcome but never welcomed.) And while it's not wrong to say something like "Comments are welcomed," it's closer to the intended meaning—and a whole letter shorter!—to say they are *welcome*.

## WHAT WITH THE

If you're going to use the retro-hipster cliche (I have to admit I'm pretty fond of it), use it right:

> *Federer hasn't had much to celebrate recently, what with the heartbreaking losses to Nadal.*

And. All. Federer hasn't had much to celebrate recently, what with the heartbreaking losses to Nadal *and all.* There is no "What with the . . ." without the ". . . and all."

(See what I did there? Word. Period. Word. Another. Hipster. Cliche.) As is "See what I did there?" I'll stop now.

# WHETHER

It's a word with "issues." Should we talk about the *whether*? Let's.

Issue No. 1: Whether "whether or not" is redundant. Or not. And the answer is . . . it is when it is. I've seen self-styled sticklers ban the "or not" in all cases, ignoring the obvious folly, but it's pretty clear that while you don't need the "or not" in "Let's see whether or not it rains today," you most certainly do need it in "I'm going to ride my bike, whether or not it rains." (Does anyone really think "I'm going to ride my bike, whether it rains" makes sense?) So delete it if you can. Don't if you can't.

Issue No. 2: Whether to change *if* to *whether*. Answer: Again, try it and see if it works. Or *whether it works*. See? Sometimes if just doesn't matter. Technically, I suppose, I should have said *whether* there. But *if* means the same thing. I don't lose any sleep over such cases. Sometimes, though, the two words express different realities. If I say, "Let me know if you want to get a drink," I'm saying I'm open to the possibility if you are. No big whoop. But if I say, "Let me know whether you want to get a drink," that indicates I'll be eagerly awaiting your reply one way or the other. The "or not" is implied.

Issue No. 3: The false dichotomy. As you may know, I tend to discourage the *false range*. It's fine to say "from Los Angeles to New York" or "from A to Z" or "from soup to nuts" because these are actual endpoints on an actual continuum. But if you say you've read everything from *Slaughterhouse-Five* to *Fitness for Dummies*, you're just tossing random titles at me in an attempt to convey the idea of "a wide variety." How is either of those books an endpoint, and

what in the world would be the midpoints? *Everything* compounds
the problem, because clearly it's hyperbole.

The false dichotomy is a cousin, and you'll hear it a lot in ad-
speak. You'll love this airline whether you're on a quick business trip
or a week-long vacation with your family. (So I guess you'll hate it if
you're going skiing with the boys or sneaking away with your mis-
tress?) You'll benefit from our financial-planning services whether
you're a corporate executive or a janitor. (Those are my only options? I can't be a cowboy or an astronaut or a ballerina?)

# WHILE

If you're still objecting to the use of *while* to mean *although*, you're
even more of a fuddy-duddy than I am.

# WIS., WISC.

*Wis.* is the standard abbreviation for Wisconsin. *Wisc.* is an abbreviation for . . . *wiscellaneous*, I guess.

# WITHOUT FURTHER ADO

It's a ridiculous cliche. Even when you don't make the mistake of
spelling it *adieu.*

# THE WRONG AND THE INCORRECT

*The wrong*, as in "You bought the wrong kind of bread again, honey," is an idiom. It usually means something more like "a wrong," but nobody says it that way, and that's fine. Remember when Jane mentioned to Aaron that "they used the wrong missile graphic"? No? Well, maybe you're not as obsessed with *Broadcast News* as I am. Anyway, she didn't mean that there were two graphics and that *the* wrong one, as in the only one that possibly could have been wrong, got used. She simply meant that the one that was used was wrong. Now, there are times when there *are* only two alternatives, and therefore the wrong one really is *the* wrong one, but I'm not talking about those times.

My point here is that the idiom doesn't carry over to *incorrect*. I guess you could say that the incorrect graphic was used, but it's better to say *an incorrect*.

## Epilogue

I suppose it's clear by now that I'm nuts. But we all are, in our own ways, aren't we? Language is integral to life, and yet no two of us speak precisely the same language. We're bound to have feelings, some of them strong, about those countless differences.

When I read the anti-rant rants of reformed language peevers, I think of the Woody Allen character who says: "I used to be a heroin addict. Now I'm a methadone addict." There we are, the still-peeving with their addiction and the reformed peevers with theirs. And here I am, apparently zonked out on both heroin and methadone, an editor in search of a fix. The learned linguists' clean and sober tolerance has its appeal, but I'm only human. I'll sound like a junkie and a pusher if, say, you refer to having a Facebook account as "having a face book," but I'll sound more like a 12-stepper if you start ranting about a dictionary's inclusion of "bromance" and "man cave."

I'm not a religious person, but the 12-steppers' serenity prayer can be edited into a pretty handy pocket guide for language snobs: Correct what you can. Accept what you can't. Be smart enough to know the difference.

# Index